MINIMALIST BUDGET:

The Realistic Guide That Will Help You Save Wealth, Manage Personal Finances and Live a Healthy Lifestyle (Minimalism, Mindset and Money Management Strategies)

Table of Contents

Introduction

I want to thank you and congratulate you for purchasing the book, *"Minimalist Budget"*.

The book discusses minimalism in detail and also provides an overview of micro and macro economics so that individuals or families can use relevant concepts to manage their finances on a day to day basis. Case studies and practical examples are mentioned so that you can see how such concepts are applied.

Thanks again for getting this book, I hope you enjoy it! If you do enjoy it, can you please leave a positive review on Amazon? I would greatly appreciate it.

Chapter 1: Minimalism and the Minimalist

Some think of it as a philosophy, a school of thought. Others think of it as a style, a way of living or a culture. Whatever you choose to think of it, it does not matter. What is important is our perception of the values of living the life of a minimalist. Our primary concern should be what we arrive at when we compare our lives as minimalists to what they used to be before we were minimalists. The question we need to ask is: "What is minimalism?"

What is minimalism?

Minimalism is an idea that can be used for good living. It is a tool that leads to blissful liberation from whatever fear has come to plague the human population over time. It also offers freedom from the very world we have created about ourselves as consistent consumers. It allows us to stop worrying about everything; we have a choice to take control and become fulfilled. The state of our purse, health or lifestyle can give us freedom from depression, from the oppressions that nag at us because of our covetousness and insatiable desires, from feeling guilty over things, either justified or not. It is a new kind of liberty and is not a consequence of our state of wealth, health or status in society. It is a subject of contention that does not limit your ability to do more. It is rather a relative idea that differs from one individual to another.

Minimalism is not a way of life because it does not stop you from being who you are. Neither does it stop you from having what you already have. Our problem in the world today is the way we see the things around us and the extent of our desires. We worry so much about everything at the expense of our health, passions, personal growth and greater contribution to the betterment of humanity. We want to own a house, and it must be a mansion. We want to have a car, and it must be a Cadillac. We want to have a family and a career, do what families do and be established. We want to be this and we want to be that. These are all very wonderful things, and minimalism is not about not having them. It is not about not doing all this, and it is not about not being what you want to be. Minimalism is simply about making these decisions and taking these actions more carefully and more consciously. It is about living a lifestyle in which regret is greatly reduced, if not eliminated. Minimalism is the closest you can get to a perfect life.

A misunderstanding among many people is that minimalism is about a lack of material wealth. That is, as a minimalist, you are free of the desire to own material possessions. They see it as a life of immaterialism. This view is a fraction, albeit a tiny one, of what minimalism is. While some minimalists have chosen to forfeit a material life, many others are material minimalists. Although it is desirable as a minimalist to be somewhat immaterial, this does not mean there is something inherently wrong with owning material possessions. The point is not to think of minimalism as just getting rid of stuff, not buying anything new or not owning property. Minimalists lead disparate lives. Some live lives of affluence, while others live on low incomes. However, there is no such thing as a poor minimalist. This leads us to the next question: "Who exactly is a minimalist?"

Who is a minimalist?

A popular myth is that a minimalist is somebody who has forsaken the love of material wealth and chosen to live a secluded life. This is not a universal truth but a fraction of a whole. A minimalist is simply someone who worries about nothing. The individual has realized the extent of his or her desire and knows that the cost of chasing such vanity is not worth it.

A minimalist is someone who has rid himself or herself of life's excesses (of numerous desires) and has chosen to focus on the necessities. The ultimate goal for such a person is to find happiness and fulfillment, and to be free. A minimalist is not discontented with his or her lot. Rather, the individual focuses on maximum output while still using available resources at a reasonable level.

The joy a minimalist feels is incomparable. This is one person who has reclaimed time. The person lives his or her every moment, reveling in the bliss of a contented life. He or she is free to pursue different passions because there is more control over life. The person is not living the life of others and can discover his or her mission and experience the true reality of freedom. A minimalist is a creator and not a consumer, although not in the perfect sense. The reality of who you are depends on the balance between being a creator and a consumer. For a minimalist, the creation aspect outweighs the consumption aspect.

Minimalists can rid themselves of almost all of the material clutter in life. Minimalists can determine what truly gives them joy and adds value to their lives. They ferociously guard their homes and their lives. They thoroughly scrutinize anything that finds its way into their minds. Because they have been able to develop a clear and precise value system, they are quicker at making decisions. They can adequately distinguish between things that make them truly happy and things that only give them a false sense of happiness. This clarity of mind and purpose allows them to waste little time doing things that do not add value to their lives. They become more productive and brutally efficient, which results in less time spent organizing things they do not need and frees their minds to focus on living a fulfilled life.

As minimalists, we can focus on our health because we have the time to do so. We do not worry and put pressure on ourselves. We do not waste our energy chasing desires that seem to move further away with every step we take toward them, and we do not deprive ourselves of the joy of true living. Being a minimalist gives us the chance to grow as individuals and contribute to the greater good of humanity. The great thing about being free is that we can discover our purpose in life and live a life of fulfillment. This is the way of minimalism.

Why become a minimalist?

The typical human being thinks that mankind rules the world. We have said this to ourselves so often that we have started to actually believe it. We think of the world as under our rule. The bitter truth is, "the world rules us!" The world is a chessboard and we are the pieces being moved around on it. If the world rules us, the question becomes "how?"

There are two ways people are owned, or two ways they are controlled—through the emotions of fear and desire. People are slaves to whatever or whomever they fear. People will go to any length to fulfill their desires. Consequently, to get people to do something, all you need to do is to either scare them into doing it or to make them desire it. Let's look at our lives and ask these questions: Why do we work? Why do we obey the law? Why do we fall in love? Why do we get an education?

Whatever the answers we give ourselves, they all point in the direction of either fear or desire. Is this the way the world should be? The answer is no. However, this is exactly what we have made the world into. We created, invented and built a lot of things that have come back to enslave us, either because of our desire for them or because we fear them. We should enjoy the work of our hands, not fear it. We should desire things but not want them so much that our failure to get them puts us in a state of misery or sadness. This is the goal of minimalism.

You cannot be enslaved if fear does not rule your world. Having less desire for material things puts you in control because you will not be influenced greatly by those material things. This is the way it ought to be. This is the real way of living. In truth, a significant percentage of the world's population is not minimalistic. This is exactly why being a minimalist is a great advantage.

So, why should we become minimalists? It is simply because we do not want to be slaves who are actually disguised as free human beings. We do not want to live the rest of our lives in fear, worrying about things that will not matter in the end. We must live like minimalists because we want to be free.

We must understand that poverty will become apparent when our available resources are not enough to match our needs. The situation worsens when we consider our wants or desires. The denial of the needful is undesirable but not enough to complicate our lives. The longing for what we want is what makes poverty harmful to us. We begin comparing ourselves with those above us. It is human nature to do this. We do not look at people below us; nor do we look at people around us. Mostly, we look at people above us and feel dejected that we are not doing enough. We feel discontented and put ourselves under the pressure of wanting to do more, wanting to own more and wanting to be something more than we are.

We feel like small fish in a large pond and strive to become part of the larger fish because their situation seems better. The goal of minimalism is not to make us feel like big fish in a small pond full of small fish. The goal of minimalism is for us to be fish in a pond full of both big and small fish and still live our lives independently of the state of the other fish around us.

What if I am not a minimalist?

"To be" or "to not be" has always and will always be a choice intrinsic to individuals, irrespective of the influence of what or who is around them. The influence of the external environment matters only to a certain extent. In the end, the actions we take are always a result of the choices we make. We are who we choose to be, whether consciously or subconsciously. Not being a minimalist is to mock freedom, which creates a funny situation given that we all like to think of ourselves as being free. The truth is, no one can force you to be a minimalist. It is a decision that you must make within yourself and for yourself alone. Ask yourself: Do I want to be free? Do I want to be happy? Do I want to let go of my fear and desires so I can become who I truly am?

What is there in being a minimalist, after all? It is nothing more than becoming a better you. If being a better you is not enticing enough, you need to stop complaining about stress. You need to stop blaming others for your feeling of insecurity. Ultimately, you must accept that you are not happy because you choose to forsake happiness. Do you really want to keep chasing what is not meant to be?

How do I become a minimalist?

Look around you. Do you feel like something is missing? Are you happy? If yes, why do you need to worry? You must already be living the life of a minimalist. If not, can you do something about it? Answering these questions will help you reduce worry and cause you to take action.

As a minimalist, you do not have to worry about life unnecessarily. If you feel your life is at a point in which what you want is what you have gotten, you do not need to worry. On the other hand, if you have the feeling that something is missing, it becomes a question of what you can do to remedy your situation. If there is nothing you can do to remedy your situation, you obviously do not need to worry. It is something you desire, but you do not have the means and resources to attain it. Even if you know something you can do to fix the situation, you still do not need to worry. Just get your wits together and start doing it. This is the philosophy of minimalism. This is how you can become a minimalist.

To become a minimalist is not merely the dissociation of the self from desire, fear and material possessions. It is to choose a life in which the absence—or, conversely, the presence—of these things does not matter. These things have simply stopped being a determining factor in defining who you are. So long as the way you live does not threaten your survival, you are learning to live the life of a minimalist. Know that the world is not about what people think of you; it is more about what you think of yourself.

Chapter 2: Individual Financial Management

The basic aim of financial management is to increase an individual's economic value or worth and ensure that it is maintained for a long period. This is why financial education is essential for everybody. Individual financial management involves applying proven financial strategies to the everyday life of an individual so that he or she can achieve the maximum financial gain in every situation or objective. It involves looking deeper and modifying all or some of the financial activities an individual undertakes so as to realize the short and long-term goals.

Do you work really hard but end up never having enough? Or are you so deep in debt that you cannot pay the bills? Maybe you see all this nice, beautiful stuff on display when passing through the mall and you realize that you may never be able to afford it. You may have read countless books and experimented with different methods and approaches, but you always manage to end up exactly where you started. Does this sound familiar to you?

The management of finances is the lifeblood of a successful business or efficient individual. It is an essential practice if an entire country, economy, individual or corporate organization is to function effectively or even survive. Individuals who are adept at managing finances can handle and successfully sustain organizations. Personal finance, however, isn't a one-off; it consists of all the decisions a person or household makes regarding earnings, investing, savings and expenses.

I assure you that this book is going to change your life because the only known way to achieve financial freedom is through financial education. We recognize that every situation is unique and different; therefore, approaches that advocate just one method for fixing all issues do not work. To work more effectively with a wide range of issues and conditions, we therefore specify approaches that closely fit every possible variation or just a peculiar need. We were able to achieve this by using the Analysis, Prediction and Minimalism approach, which we like to call the APM model. If you apply the things you learn here, I can assure you that you will achieve financial freedom and personal satisfaction in no time.

This manual is interactive and shares self-evaluating techniques which will make you more involved in this tremendous change that is about to happen in your life. This is not going to be merely lists or numbered suggestions for ending your financial struggles; these are proven methods that have worked countless times and in different situations.

Causes of financial mismanagement

According to the encyclopedia, "Financial mismanagement is the intentional or unintentional management that can be described as negligent, ineffective, incompetent or wrong." There is no doubt that it reflects badly on a business or individual. There are many reasons for this mismanagement. Financial problems and the economic situation can devastate the economy and lead any business or individual into financial mismanagement.

Some examples include:

- Faulty Allocation of Responsibilities
- Neglect of Taxes, Invoices and Payments
- Deferral of Responsibilities

Many wealthy people are tied up by debts and have also gone bankrupt over the years. Many workers have become helpless and live "hand to mouth" while trying to work more jobs to keep afloat. Financial security is not guaranteed by the amount you earn or the size of your bank account; instead, the effectiveness of your management technique causes you to be rich, dominating or in debt. People make the mistake of looking only at immediate success and forget that it is not necessarily the case forever. Let's look at a case study of Mrs. X and identify some causes of financial mismanagement on her part.

Mrs. X is an analyst who works with one of her country's major multinational organizations. She has a giant five-figure monthly salary that offers her the luxury of a pleasant and well-furnished home in the suburbs, and she drives two cars that are the latest models of their brands. Because of her position in society and of course her attractive salary, she is a member of several charitable organizations. She is married and has two children, and her husband is also paid well. Her children attend one of the best schools in the area, which brings its own financial burden. Everything seems to work smoothly for them on the surface, but not many are aware of the constant fear that lurks in their minds. Others do not know about the arguments that occur between Mrs. X and her husband about their imbalanced finances.

She hoped her job promotion would increase her six-digit salary. It eased the burden of her debts for a while, but soon she became more indebted than before because she quickly yielded to the logic of raising her family's standard of living to meet their new status. She faces a dilemma now because she was one of the people released at work during the last downsizing program. Her children have brought home a note from school stating that they would be unenrolled if they didn't pay the tuition on time. Her mortgage is due, and she has received telephone calls from one of the bank managers from whom she received a loan. (She had used credit to finance her costly lifestyle when her husband lost his job a few months ago and went into debt as well.) The bank had bothered them with messages like "interest is very low," or "you can pay at any time without pressure, and with your salary I am sure you can pay it back at any time." Hell was now unleashed and their world had crumbled.

How would she get through this? Even her possessions weren't worth as much as they had expected. Mrs. X was officially bankrupt and had no one to turn to. Then she remembered her friend and neighbor, Mrs. Y, who earned less than Mrs. X had, and who had been dismissed at the same time. However, Mrs. Y seemed fine, not overwhelmed by any obvious financial strain. Mrs. Y told Mrs. X about a principle called "Minimalism." Mrs. X had known about it before. Her friends with whom she attended tea parties had heard of her situation, and she had been left out of all charity events. Her life was now ruined, and suicide seemed to be the only way out.

The above story is not real, but was painted in the extreme case. This has been deliberately done to deal with all possible financial failures that people face so that everyone can relate in one way or another. As promised earlier, this book will be as interactive as possible. Therefore, I would like you to take a pen and paper or use the note editor on your phone, tablet or computer to indicate what you think led to Mrs. X's financial situation. This will serve as an assessment of this case study. Sometimes helping others paves the way to our salvation.

Listed below are the revised causes of financial management. You can now mark your answers here:

Financial ignorance

One of the biggest problems that can affect people is ignorance. If you did not prevent the problem, there is nothing you can do about that now. However, you can take steps to resolve the problem. If you do not know whether what you are doing is wrong or not, as in the case of Mrs. X, there is little or nothing you can do. You might take the road of condemnation. The only known and proven solution to ignorance is education. Therefore, the only solution to financial ignorance is financial education. You may not know that you are making bad money, although you know there is something called management. If you are in this category, you may want to take notes because the solution will be discussed in the following chapters.

Expansion/Procrastination

Another sad situation is a lack of knowledge about what to do now and what to delay. There is a popular saying: "Time doesn't wait for anyone." Dilly-dallying is an expensive habit. You must make hay while the sun is shining because you have no control over some circumstances. Do not relax into thinking you have control over what is going to happen. It's better to be equipped with the necessary techniques than to fall into poor financial management due to procrastination. Start now!

No perspective

While some people strive to achieve their goals, dreams or passions (to be someone, to do something or go somewhere), others do not have a clear path for their lives. They live light-heartedly and take the day as it comes. Having no ambition or plans is another way to lead a catastrophic and irresponsible life. People with clear ambitions and firm goals do not live light-heartedly. They are constantly inspired by these dreams to improve their situation so that they can make plans about the future. Living a life without prospects, as Mrs. X did, is a mistake. You can identify yourself as such a person if you do not relate your daily spending habits with long-term implications.

Your Neverland is not so far away. It's knocking on your door. Or do you think your work will last forever? You are temporarily blinded by the obesity of your salary, you live unconsciously and you spend more than your salary. You are often blinded by the monstrosity and apparent regularity of your income and do not plan according to your earnings. If you do not rectify your situation, you will face immediate problems when or if your source of income is cut off.

<u>Short-term prospects</u>

The future is determined by our present. Ask yourself: What are your goals? Do you have short-term or long-term goals? You may have increased in the "one-inch perspective" category, but are you sure this is not in the "short-term outlook" category? We live many ideological practices in the present. The future will take care of itself. Forget that life is more deterministic than stochastic. The targets are only short-term if they do not consider their long-term financial stability. You are living short term if you will have problems after a few days or a month (should you be suddenly fired or face an emergency) and have little or no savings to fall back on. The principle of spending more money than what you are earning is called overdue gratification. You must meet your goals over a 20 or 30-year period so that saving becomes a necessary sacrifice and not a burden.

Higher spending and lower earning

One of the best ways to swim in debt is to spend more than you earn. In life, we are confronted with various distractions that are fuelled mainly by envy and our need to be recognized, or to live in a way that matches what the media shows us. The concept of consumerism is:

- ✓ To buy more
- ✓ To achieve more
- ✓ To belong to a certain class
- ✓ To have fun
- ✓ To make impulse purchases, etc.

These are fast and easy ways to deplete your resources and drown yourself in debt. This is not our fault, mainly because many companies tailor their advertising campaigns to promote this lie ("you need more success"). Steve Jobs achieved this with Apple Inc. If you own an Apple product, it gives you class, which is not necessarily a bad thing. However, people who cannot afford to own such devices are making a false statement about their financial success. Luxury goods and services such as brand-name bags, shoes, make-up, cars, telephones and electronics also follow this approach. Celebrities are put on display and are made into role models. Some people who are watching become trapped in a web of lies to finance their fake lives. They get a false sense of accomplishment when they consume these products or services.

Mrs. X falls clearly into this category because of the mentality of materialism and a false sense of belonging. One thing you need to know is that you cannot get a financial boost if you earn little. She wanted to carry a heavier load than her pay check would allow. It is not a crime to have friends or to be part of a social gathering or to donate to a charity event. But when making any decision, the reasoning should be assessed thoroughly. Buying more than you need, buying on impulse or getting what you think is cool is not a good method.

Some marketing teams are now using a certain method to convince consumers who need a product or service. They will use sweet language to engage vendors with high power and cultivate them carefully to push their consumer goods. Since we do not want to be in this category, remember that sacrificing the present for now will often save the future.

<u>Lack of discipline</u>

An undisciplined person will soon fall into ruin. Discipline is the bridge between goals and performance. Thomas Huxley said: "Perhaps the most valuable result of all education is the ability to make yourself do the thing you have to do, when it ought to be done, whether you like it or not; it is the first lesson that ought to be learned; and however early a man's training begins, it is probably the last lesson that he learns thoroughly." If we reflect on the previous case study, we can deduce that Mrs. X had no discipline because she must have discovered at some point that she was overspending. However, just like a drug addict, she had become addicted to shopping, and no matter how hard she tried, she could not stop spending.

Discipline empowers the desire to save, plan or even implement your effective management techniques because you are always looking for instant gratification. In other words, you are only considering the present and ignoring the future. Are you going to a shopping center because you hear voices that exhort you to do so? Are you trying to satisfy all your desires and forgetting that your day-to-day life is paramount? Then I am afraid you are falling into this category. Discipline is a function of the mind. Only you can solve your lack of discipline by overcoming the urge to spend impulsively or excessively. This will be discussed in the following chapters.

Complex/Unsustainable budget

Many books or methods of financial management focus on financial planning, but resort to the prescription of a single method for all. Sometimes they use a method that is so complicated, it is not sustainable in the long run. Many budgeting techniques have left people worse than before, as they are soon skimming their savings and falling into debt. Therefore, it is not just budget that matters, but the right kind of budget. Make sure your budget is right for your finances. Understand who you are and the methods that work best for you. Consistency is the key to continuous improvement.

Wrong investment

This is the only part of the equation that requires financial skills. This category has hooked a lot of people. It is not complex and there are simple solutions. However, it remains the only excuse that legitimately makes a good fortune when everything else is done right. There are many situations, but those listed below are common.

1. Some fall into this category because they are victims of the short-term or non-perspective phase. They realize they are not paying attention and that their time is almost up, so they begin to panic and become the victims of bad investments. Examples include people who have borrowed money from Ponzi programs or have released their hard-earned money into liquidated shares or failed investments. As a result, they are forced to go back to the starting point with nothing to show for their efforts.

2. Another situation is caused by impatience and greed. These people have the money needed for investment, but they don't seek the correct information or review the situation before they make the investment. They proceed without checking, or they swallow the hook, line and sinker, believing the lies of friends and wolf advisors who have taken advantage of them. Some people fall through financial ignorance, hesitancy, short-term prospects and lack of discipline. This is the most painful thing that can happen to any person after he or she has saved for a rainy day only to have the funds disappear because of a bad investment.

Most solutions in financial planning involve the sale of investment products, which are the worst options for pensioners or retirees. The fear of investment leads to consultation with so-called experts, who add more misery. In conclusion, investing can be used to manage finances.

<u>No plans for contingencies or emergencies</u>

It is a well-known fact that life is not a bed of roses because you cannot expect everything to work as you want it to. Life is a roller coaster and is full of ups and downs. Even white snow with the purest heart can become a victim of evil magic. Many people have the right perspective but don't have an emergency plan. Therefore, when planning, you should always consider the possibility of an emergency or contingency. Emergencies include:

- ✓ Accidents
- ✓ Natural catastrophes
- ✓ War
- ✓ Unexpected expenses
- ✓ Health complications, etc.

A big mistake in anyone's budget is the exclusion of unexpected expenses, which would raise their ugly heads only at unexpected times. Hence, they are referred to as "unplanned." Although planning does not necessarily achieve success, if you have a contingency for unplanned expenses, you will be better off than if you didn't.

Debt

Debt may be defined as a quantity of money owed by a person or a group of people to another person or a group of people. Most debts are caused by financing a lifestyle above the average, but some are due to the arrival of unforeseen circumstances. Overall, a lack of planning and foresight is usually the main cause of debt.

The debt trap is created in various ways:

> Stranded investments
> Bad deals
> Fraud
> Loans
> Self-created methods like an extravagant life

The bottom line is that these are the causes of debt, or we can say that they are some of the indicators of financial mismanagement. Many have fallen into debt due to unsuccessful investments. Some unfortunately also jeopardize their retirement income and have little or no return. When you are unsure about an investment, it is recommended that you save your money because of the risk to all participants.

Loans are directly linked to debt. Loan agencies, local banks and micro lenders all leverage the ignorance and despair of the borrowers who ignore the full effect of the enormous interest they may have on a loan. The problem occurs when the time comes to pay back the loans. They become victims of panic attacks or health conditions and soon look for other loans to cover their current loans. Therefore, people should be careful when taking out loans by examining the terms and assessing their ability to pay them off on time. In fact, the minimalistic approach advocates a full credit life, which will be discussed in the following chapters.

Ms. X's misfortune was caused by a massive debt. She was up to her neck and she had to ask for loans to save face. This is the biggest mistake one can make. If you are in debt, stop taking on more debt to spare your neck. More debt makes things worse! Remember, immediate satisfaction is not the plan; rather, we seek future enjoyment and stability. Now, more than ever, we must plan and embrace the minimalist approach.

<u>Indulgences or bad habits</u>

Bad habits and indulgences are also causes of financial mismanagement. These habits become uncontrollable and should be eliminated as quickly as possible. Examples include gambling and excessive purchases of sweets, meals, luxury goods or electronics. Stop spending excessive amounts of your hard-earned money on these things. Stop your habit as soon as possible because the sooner you remove it, the better your finances will be.

Steps to successful financial management

The goal of a successful financial management plan is to manage your money to achieve personal financial satisfaction or long-term stability. There is a recommended six-step process that is described below:

1. Determine your current financial situation
2. Create financial goals
3. Identify factors that affect your financial goals

4. Keep the time factor in mind
5. Plan for unpredictable financial needs
6. Assess living conditions
7. Develop a strategy
8. Measure and analyze your strategy
9. Make investments

Determine your current financial situation

In this step, you will answer the questions: How and on what do you spend your money? It does not have to be a rigorous exercise to carefully analyze how and on what you spent your money in the past three months. Determine your current financial situation regarding your income, savings, cost of living and debt. Prepare a list of current balances of assets and liabilities and the amount you spend on various items to form the basis for financial planning. Separate them into clear titles such as income, expenses (rent, bills, unforeseen expenses, etc.), savings, investment (if available), debt and any other revenues or obligations.

Example:

In the next two months, Miss Jane will complete her bachelor's degree with a specialty in business management. She has worked part-time in various sales positions. She has a small amount of savings at the bank ($1,700) and over $ 8,500 in student loans. What additional information should Jane have to manage her personal finances?

Create financial goals

After analyzing your current financial situation, the next step is to set clear goals for yourself. Record the history of your financial success goals. When you set your goals, you have a blank page to write what you want, or the wheel to control your boat in any direction you desire. Knowing what you want is a desirable feature. It is important to have goals because they guide and motivate you to learn more and do more. Goals serve as a driving force.

Goals should be divided into two categories: short and long-term goals. Your two goals should work with you to help with unforeseen events. For example, your savings should be able to keep you going for a period of three to six months after losing a job. Our goals differ and relate to us as people and where we are in our lives. They push us to be better and make us extraordinary. Make a list of your long-term financial goals and remember stability matters more than immediate satisfaction. This is not like you want to save money to buy a car or build a house; no, it's bigger than that. It's the opportunity to buy a house or a car that will not be financed.

You should regularly analyze your financial values and your attitude toward your money. The analysis of your values involves the distinction between the beliefs you have about money and how these beliefs let you act in a certain way. For example, do you think it's wrong to ask for money or get consumer goods like expensive clothes? Because of this belief, you can buy clothing only once you have saved enough money for it. You would also not charge clothes to a credit card if you acknowledge that you do not have the money to pay the bill.

You should be aware of your attitude toward money. Do you see money as a kind of security? If so, it is likely to be a decent economizer. If you see money as a way to satisfy your immediate emergencies, you could be an impulsive donor. What your goals reflect is a change in your attitude. Think long-term thoughts and think like a manager; setting goals is the first step in planning.

Identify factors that affect your financial goals

Did you know that analysis shows individuals with a financial plan (made by themselves or by a professional) have significantly higher amounts of savings than those who don't?

Many factors influence your long-term financial ambitions. Individual ideals and perspective about money also influence your economic goals. Other factors to consider are the time frame over which you must perform your goals, the type of business requirements that drive your targets, and your life experience. Some of the factors are discussed below.

Keep the time factor in mind

What are you doing tomorrow? This topic involves setting goals. Short-term targets are goals that are achieved within one or two years (for example, saving for the holidays or paying small debts). Intermediate targets have a duration of two to six years. Long-term objectives include monetary systems of more than four years, such as sequestration provisions, university or education funds for children, or vacation expenses.

Long-term goals should be prepared in coordination with short and medium-term goals. The determination and achievement of short-term goals are often the springboards to pursuing long-term targets. For instance, saving for a deposit to purchase a house is a short or medium-term goal that can serve as a basis for a long-run target, such as getting your own home. The frequency of the objectives is another component of the business planning process. Certain goals, like holidays or cash for gifts, can be set periodically. Other aims, like higher education, a vehicle or a home, are less frequent.

Plan for unpredictable financial needs

The goal of getting professional coaching is inconsistent with the aim of keeping the money to pay a six-month auto insurance dividend. Consumption of materials usually takes place and includes things that are used relatively quickly, such as meals, attire and entertainment. These purchases can have an adverse impact on your finances. Sustainable product goals typically include costly items such as cars and sports equipment because these are physical elements. On the other hand, many people are not aware of non-material purchase goals. These goals can be linked to private relations, well-being, education and recreation. Setting goals for these living conditions is also essential for your overall health.

Assess living conditions

Personal determinants such as income, personal beliefs, age and household size influence your austerity measures and how you spend money. Fifty-year-olds usually spend their earnings differently than younger people do. As our society changes, different uses for money will continue to develop. Nowadays, people tend to marry at a later age, and many households have two incomes. Single parents may have several houses. We are also living longer. The family situation and the financial needs of an adult have a significant impact on activities and monetary decisions.

A "normal" person goes through four basic steps of personal financial management. At the beginning of life (until the mid-30s), the focus is on the establishment of an emergency fund to pay for a house and if necessary, for life insurance. It is often also the time to make sure you start thinking about retirement because the sooner you start, the less you will need to save in following years to catch up.

In the middle years (the 30s), the main reason behind acquiring wealth is to pay mortgage loans and increase your savings and investment. In the mature age of our lives (the 50s), when you usually get a larger income, the main goal is to create a suitable retirement fund. Finally, in the years of retirement, the focus is on the effective management of wealth that was previously acquired.

The situation in your life is also influenced by your family status, size and employment, as well as events such as:

- ❖ Education level
- ❖ Engagement and marriage
- ❖ Birth or adoption of a child
- ❖ Career change or geographical shift
- ❖ Dependent children have left the nest (i.e., home)
- ❖ Health changes
- ❖ Divorce
- ❖ Retirement
- ❖ Death of a spouse, relative or dependent

Develop a strategy

This is the most important step in planning, after setting goals for yourself. You must interpret the objectives in the applicable programs and design a sustainable strategy for yourself. It is not enough to set goals; you must also plan how to put these goals into practice and try to meet them in a focused and determined way. You need to develop a technique to highlight your goals and be diligent in following your plans.

Measure and analyze your strategy

Financial management is a dynamic process that does not end when you perform a specific action. The tasks of a manager include monitoring and reporting, so you need to evaluate your financial decisions on a regular basis. The process of measuring and analyzing your financial management strategy is an ongoing one that involves review and restructuring to monitor growth. It is more than just a progress report. You should do a complete overhaul of your finances from time to time, perhaps after three months, six months or annually.

Changes in personal, economic and social factors can be assessed regularly. If a life event affects your business needs, this financial preparation process will provide a channel to adapt to these changes. Frequent review of this decision-making development will support you in making major changes that will ensure your goals and financial activities are aligned with your present situation. How can you improve or test the effectiveness of your plan unless you constantly monitor and review your actions? Here, we get comparisons of the expected result with the actual result and adjustments are made to the strategy. Then, final decisions are made to ensure growth and continuous improvement.

You must take the time to stop and appreciate where you are and what you have achieved. Check your mistakes, losses, failures, blockages and successes. Improve your life. Self-evaluation is important because it requires that the ideas move to higher goals. There is no hard rule that categorically dictates your plan will work properly at the first attempt. You cannot reach the desired output until after the third or fourth test. Many famous inventors failed several times before they hit gold. After they "made it," the world forgot their failures. Think of your obstacles as steps to reach your goal and use them to build the life you desire. If you have an unwavering commitment to achieving your goals, if your choices are powerful and appropriate, you will find the means to reach them.

Make investments

You must be very careful when it comes to this topic. First, do not commit to any investment if you aren't quite sure of its credibility; make sure you have the right kind of information before you engage in business. Investments are very complicated and should be discussed as such. Financial advisors say that even if you save money at a certain time, money devalues. One day you might need money with great urgency and if you sloppily transfer it, you may lose money. To avoid the scenario described above, it is often advisable to invest. Investments make your money work for you, i.e., appreciate so you can do more than you could ever do with savings alone. As for the other side, you will discover that you can also lose all your money through bad investments or failed companies. Ask yourself critical questions, such as: How many people have been successful in this plan? What is the strength of your feasibility study? Are you sure you can survive, even if the business or investment fails? This question is very important, especially if you use all or almost all of your savings; you must be sure of the feasibility and sustainability of the program.

➢ **Note:** By running through your unique technique of development, applying the above-mentioned steps, you can use any convenient way to plan, i.e., pen and paper, mobile applications, computer applications or even a workgroup, depending on your personality. The result is most important.

Chapter 3: The Human Philosophy

This chapter is about philosophy. If you find this subject boring, you can skip to Chapter 4: "Understanding Personal Finances".

Perspective

A joke was popularized on social media in which a teacher asked his class to draw a ring. All of the students drew circular objects except for Little John, who drew a square. The teacher was furious at his lack of intelligence and demanded to know what Little John had in mind to have drawn such a thing. Undaunted, Little John replied that he had drawn a boxing ring!

The joke ends there, although I would have loved to have known how the teacher reacted after this reply. The teacher could not have said that Little John was wrong, as a boxing ring is still called a ring. The teacher asked for a ring and he was not specific in his request, so all of the students had a right to draw a ring from their own perspectives. A very creative class would have had students drawing objects like a cylinder (the ring of a well), square (a boxing ring), hexagon (a wrestling ring that has six sides of steel) and circle (the normal ring). All of these students would have been right, at least from their different perspectives.

For everything in life, there are perspectives, and these perspectives differ from one individual to the next. Perspective is subjective; we argue based on such views—unless, of course, we lose our argument to reasoning based on better perspectives. It does not mean that our perspectives are always right, as we can be wrong in our views. This is why we sometimes lose our arguments, especially to opponents with better perspectives. Most of us have refused to develop a flexible mind, arguing blindly and rigidly even when it has become glaringly obvious that we are wrong. Perspective is not always about right or wrong. Sometimes it can be a weak view, so much so that we leave our point of view for others who are more persuasive, convincing or charismatic. The danger lies in discarding our weak view when it is the right view and our opponent's view is wrong. When it is the other way around, it becomes learning—that is to say, it is sometimes true that we argue to learn.

In the case of a debate (and a debate is not necessarily interpreted as a competitive formal debate but can also be a simple argument in our everyday lives) in which the subject of discussion is a matter of only right or wrong, a debater can only be correct or incorrect according to his or her perspective. Let us take, for instance, the year of a nation's independence. One could argue about the day, month or year. In this argument, you can be only right or wrong, for there is no third perspective on this topic. When your perspective is the right one, it is called the **"all right perspective."** This type of view always puts the debater on the right side of the argument. It can also be applied to logical arguments in which you are either true or false, most notably in Boolean logic. A sister perspective to this is the **"all wrong perspective,"** in which a debater can be completely wrong in his or her opinion.

Then there is the **"relative perspective."** To understand this, let us recall the story of the six blind men who went to feel an elephant so they could describe it. The first one felt the elephant's ear and claimed that the elephant was like a hand-fan. Another said the elephant was like a rope because he had felt its tail. The one who touched its body said the elephant was like a wall, and another, who felt its trunk, said it was like a giant snake. The fifth claimed it to be a tree because he had felt its leg, and the sixth said it was like a ram because he had felt its ivory and thought it was a horn. There was an intense argument on their way home and in the end, they were unable to say exactly what an elephant was. The relative view causes the debater to say a fraction of the truth because he or she only has limited knowledge of the subject. An argument between debaters with relative perspectives usually does not end with a concession. Now, let us assume that upon arriving home, the blind men explained their findings to a seventh blind man who had a more flexible mind. The blind man could offer a solution by stating, "You are all correct in what you felt. The elephant must be a big animal, so each of you felt only a part. My opinion is that the big animal has everything you felt." This would cause each man to have a broader view of the elephant.

Relative perspective is mostly narrow in its standpoint, but by using a flexible mind in an argument, we can string together other bits of facts to form an absolute truth. This process must have been what some early mathematicians unconsciously went through because today we have different methods for finding a solution to a problem. A good example is the theory of matrices in advance mathematics, in which we have the Jacobian method, the Gauss-Seidel method and the backward substitution method. In philosophy, a school of thought believes knowledge is inborn, while another argues that one's state of mind at birth is a tabula rasa, that is, in a blank slate. These are relative perspectives. Given that we did not have much knowledge as infants, we can readily agree with the school that claims the mind is like a clean state at birth. The question is now changed. Who taught the baby to determine the difference between water and breast milk? Who taught the baby to cry when it needed to be fed or needed a diaper change? Who taught the baby to manipulate us with its crying? Some knowledge is innate, while other knowledge must be learned. Relative perspectives are mostly a fraction of a whole and people must develop flexible minds so they can use this knowledge to their advantage.

Have you ever encountered stubborn people? These people have shut their minds to reasoning and insist they cannot ever be wrong in their own opinion. The challenge to this is that they are truly right in their opinions, but not completely. They have what I call the "half knowledge perspective." The relative perspective is a fraction of the whole that is right in its assertion but can be more correct when combined with additional facts.

Another example is that of two men arguing about a car. One argues that the car is a Nissan and the other argues that it is a Primera. Of course, both are right since the car is a Nissan Primera, but each argues relative to his knowledge, which is a fraction of the whole. The half knowledge perspective is different. The half knowledge perspective provides just a little knowledge of the topic, but not everything.

A smartphone can make calls, play media, take pictures, surf the internet, play games and do virtually everything a computer can do. We all know this. Now let us take my neighbor, who used a Java Nokia phone and could only make calls, play arcade games and send text messages. He argued blindly with my friend that a mobile phone could not transfer videos within 10 seconds because a video is a large file. He does not know that software applications can do this in less than 10 seconds, so he argues this way. This perspective sabotages the person with a rigid mind but has no effect on others who are ready to learn.

When we refuse to move with time and blend with the trend, we end up with an outdated perspective. These are views regarding knowledge that have become archaic. These types of views are common among elders and parents who apply the knowledge of their day to day events in the modern world. Before the 70's, the word "virus" was defined only in the biological sciences. However, the word was adapted into the computer world to mean a file that causes a malfunction in computer software systems. A typical outdated argument would have the debater insisting that a virus is a living thing. It is not that this type of view is wrong; it is just that the view is no longer as it used to be. There was a time when people argued that gas flaring was the best option for oil exploration companies, and that was why it was adopted. I accepted that then, as it was the best choice. However, modern research has shown that gas flaring is a waste of resources and is even harmful to the global ecosystem. To argue in support of gas flaring would require an outdated perspective and outdated reasoning.

Some arguments can be quite philosophical, which may not be right or wrong. A friend once said to me, "I am not concerned with whether your actions are right or wrong. I am just concerned with the philosophy behind those actions." Such views come from a personal perspective and they are views on subjects that are quite relative. A better understanding of this perspective can be obtained from looking at our different views about life. You will agree with me that no one can be right about life; we all have different perspectives on it. A person who is after wealth may consider life to be worth living while his miserable and poor colleagues may think of life as hell. There are those who think life is immaterial and there are those who are purely materialistic. Arguments on personal perspective have no ending whatsoever, for each individual has a paradigm to support his or her view. The person who claims life to be the result of hard work will want to quote a successful business person as an example. Then what happened to the lottery winner? What of the person who inherits a fortune? I believe that personal perspective is built upon an individual's experience as time passes.

Democritus had a view of life in which he believed there were small, indivisible particles that made up life. He could not prove his view, and so it does not matter in history. Very little was recorded about the views of Democritus. His view was what I call the "not proven perspective." This perspective is a subject of hypothesis and a random guess at a rational conception. Such views may be right or wrong, but judgment cannot be passed on them until they have been appropriately and thoroughly investigated and it has been established that they are either right or wrong. It is foolish to argue based on this perspective. Today, these views have metamorphosed and can be seen in idea generation. People develop a view regarding a concept and as unproven as that idea may be, they still hold onto it. Maybe the greatest but unproven perspectives ever expressed were those of Nikola Tesla in 1926. How insightful Tesla's unproven perspective has proven!

Let us take a little detour here. It took Dalton two decades to prove the existence of the atom. From 1926, imagine how far mobile telecommunication has come since Tesla's predictions. Many times in our lives, we conceive of ideas that we think are impossible. Yes, they are, given the conditions in existence today, but who says tomorrow we can't make them possible? Every day, we evolve and become better than the day before as we gain more experience. We must keep trying and keep believing that nothing is impossible. It may take a lot of time to get there, as people nowadays will rightly say that the difference between here and there is "T," which signifies time. Rome was not built in a day, as the wise will always advise. Your unproven idea of today will be proven one day. Remember, success is when preparation meets opportunity.

Some of us build our perspectives on life from what has become a way of life, or the traditions of our people. This type of perspective is what I call the traditional viewpoint. It can be from superstitious beliefs, a stout belief in the supernatural or a view gained from following the ideas of a spiritual leader. This type of view is not open to arguments. Some of our modern religious beliefs may fall under this category. These beliefs are a perspective from the fallacy of hasty generalization. This point of view grows from using a single or very few events to judge the entirety of life or a race of people. What this view fails to realize is that every event is dynamic in its occurrence. People differ, even when they belong to the same race.

Perspective and minimalism

The problem with people is their various perspectives on minimalism. Such perspectives differ among individuals such that they end up confusing the objectives of minimalism. They begin to see minimalism as a religion, belief or philosophy rather than a tool to better living. The problem that arises from this type of thinking is that it makes the teaching of minimalism seem tedious. It requires a lot of convincing, rationality and targeted attempts to sway the minds of people from the perspectives that have been impressed upon them by what they have read or been told. The thing to note is our perspective regarding ourselves. It is how you feel about yourself that matters. It is what you feel about yourself that matters.

To understand the minimalist economy, you do not need a particular perspective of minimalism but an unusual perspective of two things: yourself and financial management. Materialism or immaterialism is not the subject of minimalism; they are just parts of a whole. The one true thing that matters is your interpretation and knowledge of financial management in a larger economy. How do I stay happy if I cannot afford the needed things to survive? How do the choices I make affect my emotional state and well-being? How do I find the peace of mind to live smart and be free? This is what this book is about: How to live smart by controlling your finances and winning back your freedom.

The definition of wealth

According to the Merriam-Webster dictionary, "wealth is an abundance of valuable material possessions or resources." This is how the world has been defining wealth, albeit with a little alteration here and there. In truth, this is how we all grew up defining wealth. With time, we tie our definition of success to this, using wealth as a yardstick. Many people will move a mountain or die trying, to achieve a state in which they can be termed wealthy as per this definition. It is rather a scholastic definition of wealth. The issue with this kind of definition is that it is fed to us as we grow up through the institutions people have designed to help us understand the world in which we live. They have said it to us so much that we have started believing it. It has become our primary goal, or at least one of our primary goals. But now, we all know that some perspectives can be outdated, half-truths, traditional or entirely wrong.

The reason why we had to go through the different forms of perspective is not far-fetched. We are all students of one of these categories of perspective. We do not apply a general perspective to all aspects of our lives. What we actually do is hold different perspectives on the different aspects of life. There is always a prevailing one that we use more often than the others. This is the perspective that defines us. What this chapter is about is having a flexible mind to be able to alter our perspective to entertain the idea of minimalism as a path to an improved and better life. This is not an objective of this book, but a prerequisite to understanding what this book is about.

Early in my career, the definition given above was also my own definition of wealth. We see success and wealth as synonyms. We believe that to be successful, we must own houses and nice cars and be able to take fancy vacations. To us, these "wants" are the reality of wealth and ultimately lead to success. We are merely creating a virtual image in our mind of who we think we should be so that we become an acceptable entity of humanity. We want to feel wealthy because we have structured our perspective of wealth as an integration of the worldly definition of wealth—an abundance of valuable material possessions or resources. When we fail to meet the lofty heights we have set for ourselves, we become frustrated with who we are and what we are doing. We are discontented and we think of ourselves as not doing enough. We make irrational decisions in this state, or more subtly, we make mistakes that become our weaknesses—which then give people leverage for driving fear into us. These concerns become the death of us, for we start dying the day we stop having control over our own life.

A better perspective on wealth, however, is to view it as a fusion of three things—financial security, a strong mind and spirit, and a life of purpose. The lack of one renders the others inconsequential for being used as a factor in determining the state of wealth, if wealth must remain a yardstick for success. It takes the presence of this trio to create real wealth—the type of wealth that truly defines success. You can have all the material possessions in the world and still live in fear of things. After all, they say that money without power is meaningless. This is true for people out there but not for a minimalist. Perhaps the difference in how this relates to a minimalist and a "normal" individual has to do with the view on power. How should a minimalist view power to be free from the fear it creates?

What financial security is to living, food is to the human body. Suffice it to say that financial security is the food that keeps the body going through life's endeavors. There is no such thing as a human without wants or needs. We all have what we need and what we want, and in one way or another we try to achieve it. What makes a minimalist different is that when deciding to satisfy these needs and wants, he or she can think cautiously without creating pressure or doing something that will enslave him or her to fear. This is because the minimalist does not have desires that transcend reality. The person is living in the reality of what is, rather than aspiring for the ideality of what should be. It is normal if there is a gap between your current and future demands. Once the distance is wide enough to be termed great, there is no longer value in continuing to focus primarily on the accumulation of material possessions. We are now literally aiming to build a castle in the air. However, many people will be willing to accept the situation because to them, it is not aiming too far, but simply having big dreams. The bitter truth is that this is true. To achieve these dreams, there is a big price to pay. That price is a life of wealth but devoid of purpose and a healthy mind.

Financial abundance is desirable, but it is not a purpose. The mind that is in constant fear or that always demands more is not healthy, no matter how much financial abundance is present. To be able to know and believe this is to have a perspective like that of a minimalist. This mindset will help us understand the economy of a minimalist. Not being in constant apprehension over money gives an individual a certain peace of mind but it cannot deliver real and sustainable happiness if it is in isolation. The bliss of living begins to show when financial security is fused with purpose and a healthy mindset. Living a life with purpose is important. It is great to have a strong reason to rise from bed every morning and take actions toward achieving this purpose. To have achieved this purpose, one will feel a kind of bliss that transcends what money can buy. It requires a healthy mindset to develop a purpose and act toward achieving it. Financial security is the means through which this is accomplished.

A healthy mindset is in itself entwined with perspective. It changes as often as our point of view changes. It is hard to have a good mindset if the body's state of emotional, physical and mental well-being is compromised. The stress (physical, emotional and mental) we put ourselves through by aspiring to be something larger than what we need to be puts our mind and body to unnecessary work. The energy we should have spent on achieving purpose is rather spent on chasing the wind. It is not that the high goals we set for ourselves cannot be achieved—they can be. It is rather a question of how better off we will feel personally after they are achieved. The problem we have is that we are not concerned with how we feel about ourselves in virtually all circumstances. We are always concerned with how others feel about us. This willingness to put others' satisfaction regarding our lives above our conviction is the very thing that drives us to chase the expensive vanities we have made into our goals. The problem is that we will never be satisfied. The more we get, the more we will want.

Chapter 4: Understanding Personal Finances

Most people adopt a current account as a simple way to manage their daily cash flows. The returns on investment and earnings are paid into this account. It is also referred to as a checking account. The account is operated by the writing and receiving of a cheque, although in recent times, there have been other electronic means of operating these types of accounts.

If regular funds are coming in, (for example: a salary cheque) a direct deposit is preferable. To government agencies and employers, it is a rather timely, safe, secure and efficient means of money distribution. It is the same for the recipient because he or she finds it easy to distribute the income into different accounts. For instance, you may ask that your employer pay part of your salary directly into a savings account and then ask that the remaining amount be deposited directly into your checking account. And because you do not have access to the saved fund and you will never look at the running amount, the tendency to spend the money is not always there.

There are many electronic options for withdrawing and depositing from and into these types of accounts. One can also schedule regularly occurring payments to be executed out automatically when they are due. An example of such a regular payment might be a mortgage or car payment. You can also use the account to pay for regular expenses that have different values each month, like service charges and telephone bills. In addition, you can use debit cards to pay for goods and services. The total cost, in this case, is deducted from the buyer's account and deposited directly into the seller's account.

Because the banks are the ones in charge of account management, they approve these transactions. They also frequently (usually monthly) provide account holders with an account statement that shows all of the monetary transactions carried out with these accounts for the period covered by such statements. The account is balanced when your registrations (cheque book or electronic transactions) are reconciled with the account statement. By doing this, your bank record, bank balances and information are updated and remain accurate. Banks are not responsible for errors; it is therefore important for you to go through and ensure that the bank reports match the balances in your own personal records.

Savings

In situations that may occur in budgeting personal finances, it is possible that a gap may exist between income and expenditure, which may be negative or positive. When there is a positive gap, that is, the amount of income for a period exceeds the amount spent, the excess is available for saving. It is possible for one to keep it and use it in the future, but there is also the responsibility to protect it from suffering a loss. You can also use it to create an alternative investment. You can trade money in markets to earn liquidity value. Another option is to offer to lend the money to someone who needs it to carry out his own transactions and who is willing and able to afford an interest payment for borrowing your budget surplus. When you keep money without returns, it is considered to be idle. Such money is an opportunity given up, the opportunity being the return that such money could have earned elsewhere.

Depending on the power of the forces of supply and demand for liquid cash in money markets and the effects of other macroeconomics factors, the value your money can earn in the liquidity market varies. There is also the relationship between time, risks and opportunity costs. In a case in which you are ready to give up your liquid cash for a longer period, the borrower has a lot more potential use for the money and, thus, there is an increase in the movement of your liquidity. The increase in movement, through this liquidity, results in an increase in the value of the liquidity. However, because you have lent out money for a long time, the opportunities or requirements that may arise for you to use the money within the period become your opportunity cost. They are the money's alternative uses that you have decided to sacrifice to lend out the money. Because the loan period is long, the opportunity cost increases. The tendency of such opportunity costs to occur frequently within this period creates a risk.

Saving markets

There are mainly two markets for trading liquidity:
1. The Capital Market
In capital markets, investors deal in long-term and risky foreign exchange transactions.
2. The Money Market
In money markets, the fund is marketed in the short term and with low risk to the money.

Time limits (which are usually different), the ability of the buyer to tolerate risks and the risk tolerance of the seller in the different markets can produce various forms of trade or liquidity packaging. In investing or saving over a long period, such as for retirement or education, people tend to deal in the capital market. Its longer time limit allows one to get a higher return for the risk taken. For savings that will be used in financing consumption, the tendency is to venture into money markets mainly for a short time duration for using cash. The willingness of people of most people to take on alternative opportunity costs and risks in the case of consumption is very low. They will mostly not be willing to do this. As a result, the time for which they wish to offer their liquidity for borrowing is understandably short.

In ordinary terms, the lender or seller of liquidity is the person who saves money and is willing to lend it out for someone else's use to generate a return. The borrower of such saved money is a liquidity buyer.

Savings institutions

Most people access money through banks, which act as a medium or platform for the seller of money (saver) and its buyer (borrower) to meet and transact. Banks locate and screen potential borrowers and manage the process by which the loans are repaid. Banks also guarantee that the money saved will earn a return. As such, the bank takes on the risk associated with lending. The bank can provide the consumer with a cash surplus from the sellers and then organize a feasible and standard means for the return of the money for the borrower.

The bank can also provide a service for reviewing borrowers to reduce the risk and manage and ensure loan payments. As a result, there is a reduction in risk, and the bank can attract more sellers, creating numerous offers. With more experience and diversification, banks will ultimately reduce the costs of loans and liquidity. Because they create value on the market (cost reduction), banks remain the go-between for sellers and buyers in the money markets.

Banks offer different advantages for borrowers and lenders. Authorization for borrowed amounts is flexible and varies for the duration of different loans. This means you have freedom of choice in determining how much of your liquidity you are willing to give a borrower and for how long you are willing to let it run. The bank has the right to "separate" the lender and the recipient, which makes it very flexible. Because of its ability to suit an appreciable number of lenders and borrowers, the bank can diversify the demand and supply for liquidity and, as a result, create a lower risk in the financial market.

There are many types of banks, depending on the type of money the bank generates. These differences are less pronounced when the banking sector merges and gears its collective efforts toward providing more general services. Recently, the decline in banking regulation and the rise of technology and globalization have contributed to this trend.

The three major types of banks are:

1. Retail banks concentrate on consumer savings and debt.
2. Business/commercial banks concentrate on the operational management of cash flows for companies.
3. Investment banks concentrate on funding for companies over the long term.

There are other names for retail banks, including savings banks, thrift institutions, etc. The types of retail banks are:

1. Cost savings banks
2. Mutual cost savings banks or savings and mortgage associations (personal or public)

Credit and savings cooperatives are similar. However, they are cooperative member agencies, with depositors being their cooperative members. Apart from banks, savers have other means of saving, especially for long-term purposes. Such platforms include investment funds, pension funds and life insurance firms. The focus of these institutions and their platforms is saving for the long term. To finance living expenses, many people use mainly banks.

In times past, most intermediaries operated with the structural branch model, but in recent times, some of these intermediaries have either totally or partly morphed into online banks. The bank stands to gain economically if it can successfully adapt online technological developments and software to process savings, lending and investments. The added advantages enable the bank to attract more potential savers by allowing them to offer higher returns on investment and low service charges on accounts. Many banks now increasingly offer mobile offline and online account details access using a smartphone. Finance companies that are also intermediaries are offering services similar to these, as well.

Governments, either state or federal, regulate the activities of banks because of the impact of their activities on the flow of funds.

Examples of retail banks are:

- ✓ Savings banks
- ✓ Mutual savings banks
- ✓ Savings banks and credit associations

Savings instruments

These instruments include:

- ✓ Financial accounts
- ✓ Certificates of deposit
- ✓ Investment funds of the securities industry

There are different methods banks offer through which potential savers can keep their money until they need it for consumption purposes. The variation between these offers is usually in the type of return generated for the uncertainties risked and for the alternative opportunities lost. These, in turn, depend on the amount of liquidity a consumer is ready to offer for mediation. The amount of liquidity you offer is determined by the minimum volume of money or time duration of investing.

Those who save money by making a deposit upon request (e.g., a checking or current account) earn a low interest rate, but this allows for complete liquidity upon request. Checking accounts, which don't merit interest, are less advisable for savings. However, they do help a lot in terms of money management. Some audited accounts deserve interest, but they usually require the consumer to have a minimum balance.

There is also the issuance of certificates of deposit (CDs), which are offered to a potential saver who is ready to offer large liquidity for a stipulated period of time, during which any withdrawal made from the savings account attracts a penalty. The offer comes in different forms, which can range from half a year to close to five years. Some may also come with a minimum balance requirement. There are the MMMFs (Money Market Funds), which are savings instruments in the money market through which investors or savers can get higher returns for their money because the money is offered to investments that have higher risks than in the money market. This includes the Treasury bill, which is a short-term government debt, or a short-term corporate debt (commercial papers).

For the period of time your money remains in the account, it continues to generate interest, which, if not withdrawn, adds to the money as capital for generating more interest. That is to say, if the interest on your money is left undrawn, it is added to the capital and their collective sum generates further interest. This term is called compounding or, more literarily, money generating interest on the earned interest. The rate of principal compounding is what is meant by the APR (Annual Percentage Rate) that a savings account has earned.

The type of bank savings a saver should choose should depend on the level of APR offered and the compounding rate. There are, however, fees associated with bank savings that offer high APR and greater compounding rate, such as the requirement for minimum deposits or balances and fees charged for maintenance. The interest you earn when you save money is taxed by the government because it is regarded as earned income. Quite obviously, with automatic monthly deposits in your savings account and interest rates, there is wealth growth associated with savings.

Savings strategies

The instruments you choose for saving should ideally reflect your money (liquidity) requirements. These instruments are mostly all low risk, at least relatively, so the value of the return on saving is determined by the alternative investment opportunity forgone. The goal of a good savings strategy is to maximize your profit margin. There is a tendency for one to be caught short if more liquidity is given away than needed. This is not favourable for you, a saver or a lender, as you may have to borrow to nullify the effect of the shortfall. This means additional costs. In cases in which the prediction of liquidity requirement is not possible or if you are certain that you will need the money in the immediate future, you should opt for products that reduce your liquidity options. In cases in which your liquidity requirement for use is predictable, usually over a long time, you tend to generate wealth without taking unnecessary risks. As such, you can opt for long-term products like CDs, whose returns are on the high side.

The amount of liquidity a saver is willing to offer is affected by the expectations of the saver regarding interest rates. Savers who expect a rise in the interest rate tend to save or invest their money in short-term investments (money markets) so they can reclaim their capital quickly and re-invest it at a higher rate of return, along with the interest it generated. Savers who expect a fall in the interest rate move toward the more long-term capital market, where their earnings can be maximized for a long period before they will have to re-invest them at a much lower return rate.

Another strategy that savers use is liquidity maximization through the act of investing in different savings instruments with different rates of interest or maturity. The most common is the certificate of deposit laddering, or just CD laddering. In this case, you periodically get liquidity, while at the same time earning a high return rate. Instead of putting all your liquidity in a single investment, you create a series of investments with different maturity dates; liquidity is available at different dates over the length of the series of investments.

For instance, suppose you have a sum of $24,000 available for investment but prefer to keep at least $2,000 available for unforeseen contingencies every month. If you invest the whole amount in a CD at an annual rate of 0.5 percent, a return will be earned, but liquidity will not be available until the end of the investment period. However, you decide to invest the money by investing $2,000 every month in a single-year CD at a 1.3 percent rate of interest. After a year, all your savings would have been saved into 12 distinct CDs that mature at intervals of one month. Consequently, every month, you will have a sum of $2,000 in liquid cash. The loop can be repeated if the need to spend the $2,000 does not arise.

The expectations of savers on interest rates are also reflected in the adoption of a laddering system. Since there is an expectation that there will be an increase in the rate of return, savers would not want to venture into the presently available interest rates for a long period. It is therefore possible for such savers to ladder up a series of investment instruments with a relatively short period of return (mostly less than a year). If the opposite is the case, there is an expected fall in the rate of return. The laddering strategy is geared toward CDs with long periods of return while keeping a percentage (as small as possible) of liquidity in CDs with a shorter period of return for possible liquidity requirements.

A good paradigm of the ways by which earning and liquidity can both be simultaneously maximized, the laddering strategy becomes a viable option for most capital and money investors. Still, an opportunity cost is suffered because, to save in the first place, you must make the decision to offer up money that could otherwise be spent. The forgone alternative, therefore, is the cost of all the things you ought to have purchased instead of saving. In general, savings is often referred to as delayed spending, which is tantamount to self-denial.

There is also the strategy of creating another account in which regular deposits can be made such that there is an account, usually checking, from which your living expenditures are paid and then a separate savings account used for investment. As discussed earlier, this facilitates the direct deposit system of paying wages and salary, as part of your monthly income can be deposited directly into the savings account while the rest can be deposited into the checking account. The advantage is that this makes saving a lot more effortless, though there is the disadvantage of having to be more conscious of your spending so as not to run into debt.

Because of the tax consequences that may be experienced by a savings account, some savings accounts are segregated (e.g., education or retirement accounts). This is the act of separating accounts according to their use. This, however, has no financial advantage, though it offers a psychological advantage.

Credit

The term "credit" is used a little differently in finance as opposed to the normal sense. As a common verb, it can be used in many ways, but for finance, it is used mostly to describe an allowance for a payment to be made after the time of the transaction.

Credit is a form of borrowing, as is debt. Although mostly used interchangeably in everyday conversations, the different between debt and credit lies in both their uses and periods. Credit is used for primary consumption, such as the payment of goods and living expenses. It is also used for more convenient payment by delaying such payment for a relatively short period. Debt, however, is used for acquiring assets, and the payment extends for a relatively longer period. In summary, credit is used for paying for expenses that are recurring, while debt is used for asset acquisition.

In terms of cost, a notable difference exists between debt and credit because of the difference in their usage and periods of payment. Many people often confuse these two and end up choosing the wrong one for financing.

Types of credit

There are two major ways of issuing credit: either as revolving credit or instalment credit.

Instalment credit is issued for the purchase of consumer goods, usually by a vendor such as a department store, for a single item. The vendor must screen the applicants, as the vendor is about to bear a risk by issuing credit. The risk involved is the possibility that a borrower may not have the ability to meet the financial obligations or even repay the capital. When paying back the credit, the customers makes the payments in instalments until the entire amount has been paid. The total repayment extends to cover the actual purchasing cost and the credit cost or simply the interest.

Instalment credits can be traced back to the origin of credit, but became famous for their use in paying for consumer goods when World War I ended. It expanded when the world experienced an increase in the mass production of consumer goods such as refrigerators and radios.

Revolving credit is different in the sense that a bank or financial company issues it for a consumer to purchase many consumer goods from different vendors in different ways. There is also an extension to a particular limit, so the consumer can delay paying for the different items to different vendors. There are two ways of paying back revolving credit. The first option is to pay it back in full periodically, the other is to obtain a credit card, which is revolving credit that the consumer may not pay back in full. In that case, it incurs the expense of interest attached to the capital. The credit cycle is the period by which the revolving credit must be fully paid or the period during which the credit is extended and paid. While the balance on credit cards is not required to be paid in full, minimum payments must be made.

Credit cards are recent types of debt that became popular with the advent of computing technologies. Credit cards offer the advantages of security and convenience. In the first sense, vendors all over the world accept credit cards as a means of payment for goods because the finance company or bank issuing the credit card has already taken on the risk of non-payment by guaranteeing that the trader's money will be paid. The owners of credit cards also stand less risk of being unable to make payments for emergency purchases if and when they occur.

Because of credit cards' universal acceptance, consumers can rely less on cash, thus reducing their risk of losing cash or getting robbed. In addition, credit cards allow consumers to more conveniently keep records of their purchases by creating a record of those purchases. Competition between banks and financial companies that offer credit often prompt them to offer rewards for consumers who use them for purchases. The reward is also a boost for such consumers.

As noted earlier, the tendency to be robbed is greatly reduced when one uses a credit card. However, there are also some disadvantages associated with credit cards, such as identity theft and the opportunity for credit theft. A fraudulent consumer may extend his or her credit by making use of a stolen or lost credit card. It is also possible for a fraudster or identity thief to steal your identity by using the personal information provided by the credit card without your being aware of it. It is, therefore, very important that one handles his or her credit card with the utmost care and keeps cognizant of public announcements concerning fraud alerts. You should always check your credit card statement for possible errors or charges you didn't make. Once noticed, such errors or discrepancies should be forwarded to the card issuer for action. This should also be done if your credit card is lost or stolen.

It is advisable that a consumer not regard credit cards as an extension of his or her income. Debt must be repaid, so it is advisable to use credit cards judiciously. The alternative is to use of a debit card, which provides access to your expendable income.

Credit costs

Credit has gained popularity in today's world mainly due to the development of technology and because of its safer and more convenient processes. Consumers may forget that the credit card is not actually money they own, but rather money they borrow. Thus, there is a cost for credit. To manage these costs, one must learn to understand them.

Given the fact that a credit line exists for a short time, the associated costs are mainly due to the uncertainties involved, rather than the opportunity costs, i.e., the default risk or the possibility of payment failure. The more risk a borrower shoulders, the greater the number of credit sources become available. The fewer the number of credit sources available for a borrower to use, the higher the cost of credit for which the borrower is liable.

Provisional installment loan

There are also types of credit that are retailers offer, usually for certain purchases such as baby furniture. The cost of these types of credit is a bit difficult to determine, as the form of interest rate offered is usually not according to standard rates. While some may offer low monthly instalment payments, others offer loans that do not charge interest for the first six months. To calculate the actual rate of interest, therefore, one may have to use the relationship between value and time. In most cases, the repayment can be done in as many instalments as possible, but it is ideally paid in the shortest possible time, over a very short timescale.

Most retailers offer credit as a sales tool in the same way they offer home deliveries. This is because most consumers are either hesitant or unable to pay for the purchase of durable consumer goods if they are not open to spreading the payment over a period. As such, the retailers' operating cost of sales includes the cost of providing credit and receiving its payment, and also the cost of the risk involved. These costs are offset by the interest generated by the credit instalments. To take it a step further, some retailers sell their expected receivable instalments to firms that deal in the collection and management of credit for consumers. These firms also deal in repossessing durable goods if the need arises.

Personal loans

Personal loans are general loans that can be "unsecured," which means no collateral is required or even offered, or "secured," in which case collateral is required. Personal loans may be used to finance debt. In addition to instalment and revolving credit, another source of credit may be a short-term loan ordered by a bank or a financial institution. In terms of cost, personal loans can be quite expensive, especially when adopted as credit, and their securities are more difficult too, although this depends mostly on the loan size, the level of risk the bank is shouldering and its cost.

For financial companies, personal loans are mostly secured by holding personal property as collateral. Such a financial company might be a pawnshop or a pawnbroker. These types of loans are quite expensive and can at times lead to the borrower losing his collateral. As such, this type of loan is used in desperate situations in which a borrower has no other choice available. Many financiers offer online personal loans at very high rates of interest. This is an evolved form of charging illegal and high interest rates for an unsecured loan. The practice is called loan sharking. Financiers who do this most often resort to violence or threats to ensure paybacks.

A very popular high-tech form of loan sharking loan is referred to as a "payday loan." This is a very short-term personal loan with a very high interest rate. The amount requested by a borrower is deposited in the borrower's checking account within 24 hours. However, the payback for the amount, plus any interest it might have incurred, must be made on the borrower's next payday. Consequently, it is safe to say that the loan is like a salary or wage advance, of which a large part has been spent before it arrives. Due to the high interest involved, the actual value of the salary or its purchasing strength is considerably reduced. As can be imagined, it is no surprise that most people who repeatedly take out payday loans are unable to pay them back or keep up with payments for their living expenses. In the end, they fall deeper into debt.

It is therefore evident that personal loans are by far the costliest type of loan a consumer may use for financing his recurring expenses, as they create more risk and expense for the borrowing consumer.

Debt

As discussed earlier, debts are credits that have a long period of repayment, i.e., there is the chance to delay payment over a long period. They are used in financing the acquisition of assets for long-term purposes. As a fund management instrument, credit gives convenience and security to borrowers, while debt is an asset management instrument for the creation of wealth.

The idea is to use the asset secured by a debt financing scheme to stand as collateral for securing debt. This lowers the level or amount of risk borne by the lender, as he now has something to exchange for liquidity in case of non-payment. The good news ends here, as this very advantage of risk reduction is cancelled out by the amount and maturity of the loan. In the end, if the loan is not repaid, the collateral may eventually not be worth the total cost of the loan and its maturity. Thus, lenders are concerned at large about the default risks. Because the concerns of lenders are calculated in the cost of the debt, it is natural that such risks also concern the borrower.

There are two types of risks involved in lending: the default risk (which is the risk of not getting paid back) and the risk of interest rate (which is the risk that may occur due to not getting enough repayment to outweigh the total cost of lending, opportunity cost and earning from lending). Since the lenders must make a profit, the cost of the lender's risk must be less than the cost of the debt. Therefore, to lower the cost of debt, borrowers must lower the risk borne by lenders.

<u>Use of debt</u>

Recurring expenses are best financed through the use of credit, cash at hand or a combination of the two. The maturity of the credit used for financing recurring expenses would most certainly, in a good financial management scheme, match the life span of that purchase. It is therefore financial sabotage to finance recurring expenses with debt. Rather, debt should be used to finance long-term assets.

In a case in which a consumer finances recurring expenses or consumption with debt, the result is that the debt outlives the expenses. That is, the debt remains after you no longer derive benefits from the product or service for which the debt was borrowed. Similarly, if assets are financed with credit, the result will be high payments because you will be repaying over short periods and the time available to make the payment is not enough for the debt to have generated earnings to offset its cost. For example, the annual interest rate for a credit card is higher than that of mortgages.

Because of the significance of money and time in long-term debts, the lenders of liquidity tend to rigorously screen borrowers compared to what is evident in short-term credit. This makes the transaction cost of debt borrowing higher than that of credit borrowing. Because of this, borrowers are tempted to finance asset acquisition with credit. However, the high cost of credit should be a warning for potential borrowers, especially those who need it for asset acquisition.

In terms of availability, credits trumps debt. Credit is more readily available than debt, which makes it a very tempting source of funding. However, in terms of opportunity cost and rate of interest, it is a rather expensive source of financing.

Chapter 5: Goal Setting

If you want to budget effectively, consider the proverb "Live according to your means." You want to make sure that you budget according to your means. You cannot earn a certain amount and budget for twice that amount.

For a successful budget, follow these steps:

- Calculate your fixed costs, i.e., rent, gas, car payments, food/groceries, etc.
- Determine your savings. When you consider emergency funds, you may want to increase the saving amount. It is simple and should be sustainable.
- Create a separate balance for the budget with appropriate planning.

Remember the perpetrator whom we discovered in the first step; it is now time to condemn them to prison. Discipline is critical to the success of any program. Only you can determine whether your strategy works. Cutting is very important. The culprits are frequent restaurant meals or takeout, impulsive expenses and weaknesses like games, bags, shoes, clothes and so on. If you avoid them, you will become stronger. Plan your expenses in the balance you set aside and make sure you use no more than that amount for that month, week or day, depending on your income, whether monthly, weekly or daily. Decide that you'd rather be hungry than touch your savings. When you make this decision, you will not kill yourself with hunger! Getting rid of impulse purchases will make you financially stronger. Make sure your planning incorporates your standard "normal" spending; otherwise the plan will fail.

A better way to classify these impulse debts would be to name them "controllable expenses." Do not let your feelings rule you; check them. A good manager is a controller. Sometimes we take holidays not because we need them, but because we want to look good or make our neighbors jealous. We need to reduce this kind of spending if we do not want the oppressed neighbour to buy most of our business when we go into bankruptcy. Extreme luxury–even luxury –can wait. Online shopping can be your weakness. Then you must find a way to avoid expenses. To be a good financial manager, you must be in control of your weakness. This is not to say that you cannot buy anything, but you should not buy things simply to show off.

Economic factors that affect personal financial budgeting

Another important influence on our decisions in financial planning is our daily economic situation. The forces of supply and demand are a key factor in the determination of market prices. The economy studies the creation and distribution of wealth, and the economic environment includes institutions such as businesses, government and labour, all of which must work together for our needs and desires to be fully met.

Market forces of demand and supply

As mentioned above, the prices of goods and services are determined by supply and demand. An increase in demand for consumer goods increases their prices; an increase in demand for money increases interest rates. This price reflects the limited supply of money and the demand for it. Sometimes the price of an item cannot be affected by the forces of supply and demand even though other economic factors can affect the price. Factors such as production costs and competition affect prices, while demand and demand forces continue to work.

Financial institutions

Credit cooperatives, banks, insurance companies, trusts and investment companies are the financial institutions with which most people conduct business. Financial institutions provide services that facilitate financial activities in the economy. They accept savings, manage accounts, sell insurance and invest on behalf of others. Government agencies regulate financial activities, and the central bank has a major responsibility for the economy in general. The focus of the central bank is to maintain adequate monetary care while affecting interest rates through the borrowing, buying and selling of government bonds. The central bank also seeks to maintain sufficient resources for consumer transactions and business expansion, while consumer prices and interest rates are maintained at the corresponding levels.

Global factors

The world market is another important influential body when considering financial activities. The economy of a nation is affected by the financial activities of foreign investors, and also by the competition between foreign companies and their local counterparts. On the general level, where the export of locally produced goods is lower than the level of imports of goods from abroad, the more local currency comes from the economy of the country, while a greater proportion of the value in foreign currency also occurs. As a result, domestic consumption and investment will be reduced; this reduction could lead to an increase in interest rates.

Economic conditions

Trade journals and periodicals regularly publish current economic statistics. The economic indicators that influence your financial decisions are listed below:

- ✓ Exchange indices
- ✓ Provision of money
- ✓ Interest rates
- ✓ Trade balance
- ✓ Consumption expenditures
- ✓ Consumer prices
- ✓ Unemployment rate
- ✓ Housing starts
- ✓ Gross domestic product

Effective guidelines for goal setting

As former Beatle George Harrison sang in *Any Road*, "If you don't know where you're going then any road will get you there." Defining proper objectives is essential for making the right financial decisions as you travel down the road to your financial objective. Your financial goals are what you use to plan, implement and monitor the progress of your savings, investment and spending activities. The following important factors must be considered when setting your financial targets:

- Your financial goals should be as realistic as possible. Your financial goals must consider your life situation and income. For example, it is far from realistic to plan on buying a new car while you are a full-time student.

- Your financial objectives should be measurable. Exact knowledge of the nature of your goals will help you plan to reach them. For example, a typical goal like "I want to have $5,000 in an investment fund by the end of the next three years" is a clearer planning guide than "investing money in a fund."

- Your financial goals should have a deadline. In the above example, the target was set for three years. A timeline like this will help you measure your progress in your financial goals.

- The financial objectives should include details about the measures to be implemented. Your financial activities usually focus on the type of goal you have decided to accomplish. If your goals have value and importance for you, you will find that they are easier to reach. You must ensure that your goals are specific, measurable, action-oriented, realistic and timely (SMART). Be sure you are explicit in planning your goals and then in the type of actions you will take to achieve them. For example, "I want to save $3,500 for renovations over the next 12 months by reducing my entertainment spending and working five additional hours a week." The goal is specific and action-oriented. It is possible to measure the progress of this target within one year. If you have ultimately earned more by reducing your entertainment costs and working overtime, your goal is realistic. And you have set a timeframe (12 months) by which you want to achieve the goal. If you can reach it within this timeframe, your goal is timely.

Chapter 6: Case Study for Financial Planning

Consider the following case study. Alan and Felicity are only one semester from completing their courses at a state university. Alan received a BSc in guarding duties and is considering going on for a fire safety engineering certification course that might require an extra $4,500. With his diploma in defence services, several business areas will be available to him. When Alan applies for jobs, he wants the work to be more than just a safe job but also a satisfactory job.

Felicity holds a BSc in medical engineering and expects to have a career as a laboratory technician. She had interviews with a local medical company and a regional hospital. She wants to get a hospital job because the pay is good and she can get further training on site. Alan and Felicity both know they require supplementary certifications to ensure they have the best chance of getting jobs. And, of course, they already have debts for the costs of their undergraduate courses.

Felicity had taken a Stafford loan, with the federal government subsidizing the loan until six months after her graduation from college. In summation, it will amount to a total debt of $40,000 of principal at a fixed annual rate of 6.8 percent. In her planning, Felicity has the intention of beginning to work immediately after graduation and to take lessons at night or on the job for as long as it will take her to get the certification she desires. Devoid of governmental subsidies, this additional training will amount to an extra cost of $3,500. In her present work, she earns approximately $5,000 a year working weekends as a home health aide. This amount could easily double after her graduation from college. In addition, she qualified for an annual Pell grant, paying her about $5,000 a year for each year she is enrolled as a full-time student. From this grant, she was able to pay for her rooms in an off-campus student co-op housing unit. This is where she met Alan, who also lives there.

Alan wants to get to a position where he can propose to Felicity. He wishes to be a good father and husband. Alan received a grant from his kinsmen, supporting students from his hometown. He also received unexpected funds from selling his grandmother's house after her death in his second year at university. He has borrowed around $35,000 over his five years at university at a 2.25% interest rate. He attended part-time courses throughout the year, so he could hustle to acquire more money for living expenses and college. He makes around $19,000 per year as a caterer. Alan feels grateful for the payments his family made, which helped finance his studies. Finally, he is also aspiring to support Felicity and pay his Stafford loans as soon as they get married.

Felicity contributed $3,000 to US spokes series cash, which will grow in about two years. She also managed to drop about $600 in a clothing and gift savings account. Alan used the all his profits for books and lessons. His only remaining asset is his old trustworthy van, which he estimates to be worth $3,900. For Alan and Felicity, access to reliable transportation is a major concern for their work. Felicity must apply for public transport to get her new post following convocation. Both are clever enough to avoid using credit cards.

Alan and Felicity ought to obtain a new apartment after their studies. They have the option of renting an apartment, looking for a different collaborative home option or getting married now rather than later. Alan, however, has a free rental option to move temporarily into his brother's home. Felicity feels strongly about the economy. She wants to purchase a house. She was going to wait until she established her career before she starts with children. Felicity seems worried about a good job with benefits. such as paid vacations and health insurance. Alan wants to retire as soon as possible, although he is still very young and does not have a clear idea of how that is possible. He dreams of running his own catering business after retirement.

Felicity's wages as a basic laboratory specialist will be around $30,000. As a basic fire engine engineer, Alan would start at $38,000. Both can increase their wages after working for around 15 years, despite the economic fluctuations. Apart from Felicity's dabbling, she and Alan have never been active in the financing market. However, as quickly as feasible, Alan needs to place money in a diversified holding of capital market stocks comprising corporate and local bonds. However, the market situation influences the possibilities open to Alan. Business money is hard to find; moreover, work is very limited and competitive, loans are difficult to get, and reward schemes and inflation—which affect retirement funds—are at risk of losing value and purchasing power. It is not clear how long it will take until the trend is reversed, so they should play it safe now. Then, there is the issue of landing jobs they want. If they don't, what do they do?

Alan and Felicity have critical decisions to make. Moreover, any of their decisions have a high risk of negative consequences that can affect their lives drastically. Therefore, to make the right decisions, they need to ask themselves some very thoughtful questions. These include such questions as:

1. What are the options for Alan to specialize in the job he wants?
2. If Alan must move for his job, what are the possibilities that Felicity will get a job in the area of medical/healing specialisation that she wants?
3. What factors influence the thoughts and choices of Felicity and Alan?

4. How much will Felicity's college cost and how will it be paid?
5. How does Alan commit to paying back his family?
6. What additional training is required and how will they finance it?
7. What short-term and long-term aims do they have separately? How will they address their goals and how many commitments do they have to make?
8. What must they do about their retirement and health insurance?
9. What is their decision about savings and investments?
10. How would they plan their marriage and family life?
11. What would be their decision regarding whether to buy or rent a house?
12. Based on all sources, what will their current earnings and projected salary be?
13. What are the demands their present responsibilities place on their current income? What would happen in the future?
14. How do they plan for unexpected situations and emergencies?
15. How can they structure their budget to pay for their short-term goals?
16. How do commercial determinants influence their decisions and what are the consequences of these judgments?

The above case study was meant to bring out questions you should ask yourself. You are bound to make monetary judgments while you are still alive. You will seldom have complete knowledge of the future and hence will not be able to completely plan for whatever occurs. Things happen and sometimes you need to make a snap decision. Individual financial preparation is all about creating purposeful arrangements that enable you to continue toward your goals so that even if a financial snap occurs, you can deal with it and then continue aiming for the goal you were moving toward previously.

The concept of individual financial planning is not necessarily distinct from the concept of making a proposition on almost everything, wherein you determine where you want to be regardless of wherever you might find yourself presently, then have the ability to go from where you are now to where you want to be. This method, however, is aggravated by the quantity of determinants to be considered and their twisted relationships with one another. This is mainly because the way you support your life now affects the quality and kind of life you will live. This method is often very complicated due to the element of uncertainty it involves; you would often make decisions with a lot of information, but with less conviction or even less predictability.

Individual business operations and their movement toward a goal involves continuous monitoring and feedback. Business strategy must be evaluated, improved and modified. It must be sufficiently adaptable to respond to unforeseen demands and requests and, more importantly, sufficient to return to targets while defending against unknown hazards.

One of the most valuable means of preparation is getting the right information. Today, we live in a system flooded with lots of information, although to use this information you need to know what exactly it is, what weights to assign to it compared to other data, and even where it comes from and how you intend to use it.

Minimal factors that influence financial thinking

Each individual has unique characteristics due to the circumstances that shaped his life and influenced his thought process. These characteristics can be physical, psychological, emotional, social or religious. These all influence someone's lifestyle and are primarily responsible for his behaviour. Therefore, these factors also influence a person's monetary concerns, decisions and plans. These factors are derived from your needs and wishes and the extent to which you can meet and protect these needs, your current lifestyle and your imagined future. Strong individual monetary preparation depends on a thorough understanding of an individual's circumstances and personal goals. Although characteristics, needs and wishes differ from one person to another, there are similar and life-related events that affect the financial planning of all. They are listed below.

Family structure

Family status and relationships with children, mothers, fathers and siblings determine whether you plan for yourself or partially for other people. Assuming you are responsible for other family members, you have a monetary obligation to them, and this should be included in your business statement.

You can expect the dependency of a parent to stop at a given time (for example, you may stop helping children or the elderly at a given time). Partners and positions affect your financial planning as you try to provide for others. For example, you may be paying temporarily for your children's education.

Being responsible for others increases your needs. Responsibility for people also affects your attitude and tolerance of risk. In general, the availability and capacity to reduce risk lie with the family and the desire to make your income stable. Individuals often use the security of their capital or property, even beyond their useful lives, to guarantee the long-term cooperation of their allies and wards. A good example of this is a life insurance policy.

Career opportunities

Your professional decisions will influence your budgeting (especially educational needs), your income or potential salary, and the characteristics of the profession you choose. A career includes hours, salaries, benefits, risk factors and profiles of progress over time. Thus, your budgeting can reflect the realities of a communications employee, a star athlete, a responsible sales representative, a professional, an independent artist, a librarian, a contractor, a teacher, a website designer and so on. For example, most athletes younger than middle age face a greater risk of injury and constant control even though they have above average income. On the other hand, the careers of most business owners last longer, although with an increased risk of unpredictable income fluctuations.

Wellness

Your well-being is another factor that can influence your proposed income demands, your risk-taking and your individual business preparation. Individual business outlining must incorporate some security due to the possibility of a chronic health problem, an accident or long-term weakness, and unusual provisions for a short-term phenomenon such as maternity and childbirth. If your energy weakens your income or your ability to work is reduced, the result can drastically increase your expenses. As a result, your income needs may go up. You must defend yourself against additional restrictions or increased costs that could develop. However, at the same time, the possibility exists that your risk tolerance could be reduced, which affects your financial options.

Most people start their financial lives by getting an income from their work. When they have savings, they begin to invest and grow their portfolios. Over time, they change jobs, get supplementary jobs, move between paid and independent jobs, become unemployed and resume work. In addition to career opportunities, these changes affect individual business planning and management.

Age

Needs, values, desires and priorities change throughout one's life. Moreover, business interests change respectively. Personally, personal finance as an administration and preparation process is expected to change. Although people are diverse, some business affairs are general or characteristic of the various events of a grown-up's life. The analysis of the different stages of life is also a component of business preparations.

At the start of a person's adult life, he or she is often single, has little or no wealth and usually has a few assets. These assets could be ways to generate income, reduce expenses or save property as an expenditure. Even as an adult, there is an expectation that one has relatively modest income needs, particularly when one looks after just himself or herself. With virtually zero expenses, such people are very willing to consider high-risk income generation. However, at this period in your life, you should be ready to grow in your profession and increase your income. Any investment you make now should be focused on growth.

Lifestyle expectations are also increasing. Maybe you now have a partner, dependents, or older parents to take care of. Additional expenses will follow, and additional needs must be met. As a middle-aged adult, you will have more options: your home, a successor or even a retirement bank account.

As spending, revenue and wealth increase, so does the ability to increase risk, although the enthusiasm to do so generally decreases. Now a person has things and people to monitor: property, positions or loved ones. As the person ages, his or her mentality begins to change, and he or she sees things in a different light. The person notices the need for more protection and stops striving one day, whether voluntarily or not.

The first and middle years of adulthood are years of construction: you are concerned with building a career, building a family, increasing your revenue and expanding assets. Expenditures are rising, as are investments and other means of revenue.

The late adult age is a time when there could be limited confidence in your revenue and also in the accumulated assets, with perhaps more properties. At this point, you may require less effort, since your children are possibly adults, or you have lost one or both parents. The responsibility for other people is greatly reduced. So, your costs are lower and you tend to have some spare time, particularly after you retire.

Regardless of children or parents, spending declines. Nonetheless, you can have the freedom to satisfy your deepest desires. At some point, you have no responsibilities for others but your assets demand more protection because they are now your only means of revenue. As a rule, your ability to withstand risks is solely because of your combined assets with your partner. However, the willingness to take on risks is very low because you are completely dependent on these assets as a source of income. This reduces your tolerance to risk. Adequate financial preparation relies primarily on how you planned your present and your life phases.

Maximal factors that influence financial thinking

It's not just micro factors that influence financial thinking. A factor called macro or systematics also affects financial planning. This is because external economic factors have an impact on personal finances, i.e., inflation, deflation and so on. Therefore, financial planning must also consider other economic conditions and the markets that make up this economy—markets such as the labor market, where trade takes place through employment or recruitment and competition exists for workers by employers and jobs by workers. There is also the capital market, where the subject of trade is capital (cash or assets), mainly in the style of shares and bonds, as well as other forms of capital packaging. There is the credit market, which is also part of the capital market, where capital (money) is lent for purchase and sale. There are other markets outside those that exist in a constantly changing economic environment. Knowing this background is the key to sound financial planning.

In the long term, the growth of an economy, the return on investment and the positive appreciation of the value of money can occur over time. This is not relatively accurate for a short-term scenario in which any systematic factor occurring at a bad time or a longer period than expected could lead to a financial imbalance. It is therefore preferable to understand the economic models and factors that indicate the welfare state (i.e., the wealth of an economy) and use the knowledge necessary to make financial decisions. Some of these factors are explained in Chapter 7 (Understanding Economics). If you already know about how economies function or find this subject to be boring, you can skip to Chapter 8 (Financial Preparation) for more personal finance advice.

Chapter 7: Understanding Economics

Business cycles

An economy tends to be the most productive thing that meets the needs of its members. In general, economic performance increases as the population increases or the expectations of people increase. The production or productivity of an economy is determined by its gross domestic product (GDP) and not by the value of what is generated over a given period of time. As GDP increases, the economy continues to develop. When it falls, the economy contracts. An economy that lays down for half a year is considered to be in recession. If the recession becomes very long, then it considered to be a depression. GDP is a well-known indicator of an economy's health. Over time, the economy is usually cyclical, usually expanded, but sometimes it contracts; this is called the economic cycle. The periods of contraction are regarded as market corrections, or the market regains its equilibrium after the growth intervals. Growth is not always smooth; sometimes markets are unbalanced and require a correction. Over time, the contraction times seem less frequent. However, it means that economic cycles have still occurred.

There are many metaphors to illustrate the cyclical characteristics of market economies: "peaks and valleys," "boom and bust," "expansion and correction," "growth and contraction". Although cycles occur in a unique mixture of circumstances, they occur because situations change and the economic balance becomes unstable. That is, an event changes the balance of supply and demand in the economy. Sometimes demand increases too quickly, and the supply cannot keep up. There are countless reasons why this can happen. But whatever those reasons, sellers and buyers respond to this imbalance, which then causes a change.

Employment rate

An economy creates not only goods and services for its members but also jobs because most people engage in the economy by marketing their work, and most of them rely on their wages as a main source of income. The economy must therefore be able to acquire wages so that more people can participate in the market. If not, other people should be treated in a different way, such as through social support or charity.

The unemployment rate is a model of the weaknesses of an economy because it shows the percentage of people who are willing to work but are unable to do so because the economy cannot provide them with jobs. There is a constant rate of natural unemployment as people migrate into and out of the workforce when life situations change—for example, while training for a new career or taking time for family. But natural unemployment must always be weak. Unemployment also reveals the economy as inefficient because it is unable to provide all its human resources with productive labor.

The acquisition rate or the employment rate of the labor force shows how an economy is likely to create opportunities for the sale of labor and the efficient use of its human resources. A healthy market economy uses its work productively and offers employment opportunities as well as the satisfaction of the consumers in their markets.

At the end of maturity, the marketplace is placed in a non-sustainable situation. It develops too quickly, shows too much work or shrinking demand, and also shows very little interest in the undertaking.

If there is a significant request for work that leads to increased jobs and no workers are available to fill them, salaries will increase to cause a rise in the price of products and services. Prices tend to rise quicker than salaries that would deter consumption, which ultimately weaken output and cause the marketplace to reduce its "boom" to a humble rate of development.

In cases in which we have very little need for labor (there are many more workers than available jobs), earnings will fall. People will become unemployed or remain unemployed. If payments grow at a very low rate, employers are theoretically inspired to take on more workers, which would lower the employment level. However, this does not always work because individuals have work versatility. This means that they are ready and can move between the economic circles to look for work.

If the rate of unemployment is high and extended, there are individuals who go without pay for a long time and who cannot engage in the marketplace because they have nothing to trade. In this situation, the exchange ground in the economy will be useless for numerous individuals. This will necessitate a change.

Other signs

Other financial signs will give us a clue about the "wealth" of our economy, the state of growth or the prospect of later growth. However, these signs are possible for incorporating statistics such as the quantity of residences under construction or the sale of existing houses, the number of contracts for gains (e.g., equipment and cars), producer prices, consumer confidence, unemployment and GDP growth. However, the two common respected benchmarks must be placed at the centre of anything our marketplace needs to work. They provide various opportunities for most individuals to engage in the market to create and produce work and meet the needs of consumers by giving them whatever they want, whenever they want. A growing and prosperous economy will give members more options for labor trafficking and capital exchange. It will create additional possibilities for income or revenue and hence create further diversification and less uncertainty.

Usually, everyone prefers to engage in a robust marketplace in every situation, but it is not feasible at all times. Financial preparation should include risk planning for economic factors to influence financial sensibilities. A time of recession can increase unemployment, reduce profitability or hinder the potential for increased income. The income of employees could be collectively lost. Such a short, spontaneous loss of wage income will probably happen to a person during his or her working life, since he or she will inevitably be part of one or more economic cycles.

Coverage against wage loss is considered to be an investment that generates other means of revenue. In times of financial recession, the application of resources and their value can also be reduced. Some organizations and enterprises are seen as resistant to business cycles (e.g., medical care and public education), but overall the return on investment can be affected. That is why the economic cycles during your lifetime will also influence your commitment to resource markets.

Value of currency

The advantage of a constant currency is that it's an extra-crucial symbol of a strong market and an important factor in business preparation. However, the price of money is based on its utility. If a government offers little of what everyone wants, its money has little significance compared to other money because there is only limited application in the business. The value of a currency is therefore a symbol of the productivity of an economy.

The advantage of a currency depends on your purchasing power. The more you buy, the cheaper and more worthwhile it is. If prices increase or if something gets expensive, the acquiring power drops. This means that money buys less and its value has decreased.

If the value of money falls, the marketplace will experience a boom. Your currency is less valuable, and you can buy less. Costs are increasing. You need more monetary units to purchase the corresponding amount of assets. When the sum of money increases, an economic deflation occurs and prices fall. For instance, let's assume you can get five video games for $20. Each game is worth $4, or every dollar buys one-tenth of a game. Suddenly we have a boom and costs or expenses, including those of video games, rise. A few months later you need to purchase more games, but this time your $20 will get you only two games. The growing prices have reduced the purchasing capability of your money. If deflation occurs, costs will drop. Therefore, maybe a few months later you can buy 10 video games using your $ 20. Now every game requires only $2 and every dollar buys one-half of a game. The corresponding amount of money is now buying more games. As a result, its buying power has increased.

Inflation is often estimated by the customer price index (CPI), an indicator of inflation or deflation, which is estimated by the national average of a "basket" of basic goods and services purchased by the average consumer. The CPI is an index formulated and monitored by the government. This is an established way of monitoring the changes in prices of goods and services, and shows either inflation or deflation.

Currency fluctuations can also influence investment when the money that buys investments does not have a corresponding value that the venture had to produce. Suppose you lend $200 to a friend who agrees to pay it back in six months. There is a boom in the market, so in the months to come, the value of the money drops, which means it purchases less when prices are rising. Your companion pays you back as agreed. However, now the $200 she returns to you is less valuable because $200 now buys less than it did when you gave it to her. Your investment has lost its value when you consider that $200 can buy less.

If the price of the currency—the shares where the asset is estimated and recorded—is unbalanced, it is more difficult to predict the return on investment. In these situations, the investment includes increased risk. Inflation and deflation are both currency fluctuations that hurt a marketplace and financial planning. Unbalanced money influences interest rates or the buying power of the revenue. Cost changes could alter expenditure decisions and changes in monetary value influence investment arrangements.

It is common to believe that things remain equal over time. However, economic preparations must include the fact that you will experience business cycles throughout your lifetime. Try to assess the dangers of a financial downturn and the eventual loss of income or capital gains or the potential loss of income and salary. At the same time, try not to depend on the benefits of an economic expansion.

Chapter 8: Financial Preparation

The planning process involves a series of activities that produce a result. Therefore, a financial planning process is made up of various activities that lead to decisions about where you stand today, where you want to be and how you can achieve that goal. Here are the steps:

- Define goals
- Assess the present situation
- Know your options, evaluate those options and estimate the result
- Re-define goals
- Evaluate alternatives and make decisions
- Evaluate new options; select and evaluate the resulting situation again

Personal conditions change, just like the economy. Therefore, your plans should be resilient enough to accommodate these changes, but stable enough to help you accomplish consistent long-term aims.

Set goals

Deciding where you want to head in your business life is an objective. It requires short-term goals, which can be around two years, mid-term goals (two to 10 years) and long-term goals, which are fairly practical and the most desired goals. The objective is a profession that usually develops through background knowledge. To be beneficial, the goals should follow the SMART theory. This is an acronym for specific, measurable, achievable, sensible and timely goals. Goals evolve over time. Whatever your aims may be right now, remember this life can be complicated and precarious at times. Simply having a plan to meet your aims in life improves your chances of achieving them.

Consider the case study that was discussed earlier in this book. After studying at college, Felicity focuses on revenue to provide living expenses and bills, including student loans. In the next 10 years, she plans to have a family. If this is the case, she might need to purchase a home and perhaps begin to save for education for her child. Her income must adapt to her higher costs and also create an excess that she can save to purchase a home and provide savings.

Maybe your aim in the long run is to retire and use all your income from your acquired goods to cross the world on a sailboat. You must have purchased more than enough property to achieve your retirement and travel income. Felicity's income is used to achieve her goals, making it essential for her to be aware of her income.

Evaluation of the current situation

Determining the place where you are at the moment or simply assessing your present situation involves knowing what your current situation is and the options you can create. There could be several options, although you need to recognize those that are most useful for achieving your goals.

The estimation of the present situation involves organizing individual business data in reports that show various and essential aspects of the financial life of your debts, revenues, assets and spending. These figures are presented in financial statements, balance sheets and cash flow statements. Companies employ these three kinds of records in their financial strategies.

For now, we can evaluate Felicity's situation by separating her assets from her liabilities and structuring her annual income and expenses. This helps her anticipate a budget deficit or surplus and will reveal the extent to which her goals are possible.

Felicity's assets are a car worth $5,000 and a savings bank account with a balance of about $250. Her debts are a student mortgage with a balance of about $53,000 and a car loan with a balance of around $2,700. Her annual one-time income after taxes or home payment is around $35,720, and yearly payments should be about $10,800 for taxes and also $14,400 for living expenses—food, entertainment, clothing, gas, etc. Her yearly loan spending is about $2,400 for automobile loans and around $7,720 for student loans.

Felicity has a yearly surplus of only $400. This will achieve her short-term aim of decreasing her debt, although with little yearly excess, it will be a challenge for her to start meeting her asset acquisition goal. Because her surplus is very small, she may not have sufficient savings to match the eventuality of a future budget deficit or even an unforeseen contingency, which cannot be completely ruled out.

To reach this intermediate target, she needs to improve revenue or reduce spending to generate more than just a year's surplus. If her automobile loan is paid off next year, she may want to purchase another vehicle, leaving only about $650 as a deposit for the car. If her student loans are repaid in about five years, she might not be entitled to student loan instalments that will drastically increase her surplus by $7,720 a year, allowing her to place this money in the student's collection.

Felicity's long-term aims also rely on her ability to acquire productive assets. When she's ready to stop working, she will use her revenue red. Felicity is striving to achieve her short-term debt reduction goals before managing her interim and long-term targets. Until she reduces her bills, which would cut spending and increase her income, she cannot work toward temporary and long-term aims.

When assessing her immediate situation, Felicity can see that she will have to stop accumulating assets until she can decrease her costs by reducing her bills (plus the spending on her student loan).

Felicity knows her immediate situation from two uncomplicated areas. One is her assets and the other her bills, along with her revenue and spending.

Evaluate alternatives and make decisions

In considering how to move on from here, there are means of distinguishing current options and approaches or sets of long-term options. To accomplish this, you need to be practical and yet, in the sense of your immediate position, see the current options and future alternatives that can create your next choice. The features of your living circumstances—family structure, profession, health, age and the broader context of your financial situation—affect or determine the corresponding value of your decisions.

After thinking of alternatives, evaluate each. The clear points to look for, plus those things to evaluate, are your advantages and costs and the risks associated with the option. You may wish to have as many options as possible. You also need to have your options well-diversified. In this case, you can decide how this decision will influence your subsequent decisions.

In her present position, Felicity lowers her debt, so a decision would be to proceed. You could start acquiring assets earlier and get many them if you cut expenses to produce more than just a budget excess. Felicity watches her costs and decides she cannot reduce them very much. She has decided that a choice to reduce spending is not possible. However, she could increase her income. She has two options: working part-time or going to Las Vegas to participate in a poker game.

Felicity could operate a second job as a part-time worker, which would raise her income after taxes, but she could become exhausted and have little time for any other interests. At this point, the whole economy is in a state of crisis; the unemployment rate is rising and therefore it is likely that her second job would not pay much. However, she could travel to Las Vegas and win big at poker; her only cost would be the price of the trip. To evaluate her options, Felicity wants to calculate the profits and costs of each.

Defining Felicity's preferences in this way shows her potential results more precisely. The option with the greatest interest is the journey to Las Vegas, but it also possesses the highest cost and has the greatest risk. If she loses, she might end up with even more debt. This would mean that her ability to acquire more assets would be delayed further until she could repay these new debts and also her "normal" actual debts.

Therefore, the best route for Felicity seems to be increasing her income and reducing her costs. She must increase her income through part-time work, which she had initially rejected because of its impact on her personal life. She should probably also reduce spending, an idea she initially rejected because it is not a rational choice. The danger of the Vegas decision is that it might lead to the selection of alternatives that she had already declined as being too expensive. The alternative of Vegas will be less acceptable if her risk is integrated into the calculations of her costs and benefits.

It is clear that Felicity will lose wealth without risk as a cost; the Las Vegas option seems rather tempting and requires taking a reasonable risk. However, the high price and risk comes with restrictions that could put her future options at risk. The inclusion of risks involves not only immediate or short-term rewards, but also long-term consequences and limitations in your area of choice, i.e., the maintenance or elimination of certain options. Strategic thinking and decision-making are very relevant and are used for options that are then carefully seen under a different light. Sometimes you can choose an alternative that has a less visible benefit than others, but also has less risk. Sometimes you can select an option with a less immediate benefit, but more options later. The risk itself is a cost and the choice of an advantage must be covered in your assessment.

Basic concepts in finance

Money, as the saying goes, earns money. If you have it, it is often easy to get more. The great difficulty is to get some to begin with.

Personal finances face the challenge of getting money. It is about managing one's income and wealth to satisfy the desires of life or create more income and wealth. The aim is to create productive assets that can be used to achieve future economic benefits, such as increased income, reduced expenses or the safeguarding of such assets as an investment and the protection of existing assets. In other words, personal finance is about understanding how to get what you want and protect what you have.

There is no shortcut to managing personal finances. Making good financial decisions is primarily about learning about the economy, how money changes and how people make financial decisions. The better your perceptions are, the better your ability to plan and avoid inconveniences. Life can never be fully planned, and well-thought-out plans go wrong, but the prediction of risks and protection from them can reduce exposure to inevitable errors.

Income and expenses

According to the encyclopedia, personal finance can be expressed as the method of paying for or funding a life, plus as a means of livelihood. Plainly, a company needs to be funded so it can pay for equipment, labor, materials and running expenses. A person depends on the income from the sale of work or capital to finance costs just as a company depends on its income from the sale of goods or services. You must learn this funding method and the cycles which are used in describing it as a method. In the subsequent chapter, you will learn more about this topic.

Income is what you have made or obtained at an assigned point of time. There are several terms for income, because there are numerous ways to earn an income. Income comes from earnings or salaries, deposit accounts, savings accounts or net earnings, which could have originated from loans. The possession of a corporation or a private company entitles the holder to a dividend.

The two basic ways to profit from a market economy are the sale of labor or the sale of capital. The sale of work means either to work for another person or for oneself. The income here is in the kind of salary check. The total remuneration can also include other income, such as pension participation, health insurance and life coverage. The work is sold on the industry market.

The sale of capital means investment: Take cash and sell or lease it to an individual who needs liquidity (passage to cash). The loan is the action of leasing the capital and the interest earned is called rent. Also, you can borrow by direct agreement with your borrower. Moreover, you can rent through a known bill swap by buying a government, governmental or corporate loan. Investing in the company's shares is an instance of trading capital for part of the future value of the company.

You can also invest your money in various other types of assets, such as art, land, antiques or raw materials like live cattle, soybeans or platinum. The system is identical: The investment is to borrow capital or sell it for a property which you can resell or use to generate later revenue, or both. Money is sold and lent to the loan market, which is a critical component of the principal market.

In the labor business, the labor price is the salary an employer (work-buyer) promises to pay the operator (the retailer of labor). For a particular job, this price is defined by many constituents. The type of work determines the required skills and training and the cost can take into account other factors, before-mentioned as the situation or availability of the position.

In return, the necessary skills and appeal of the job will decide the amount or type of workforce to be provided for the particular work, i.e., the quantity of individuals who are willing to do the work and the number of people who can do the work. If the job offer exceeds the demand, i.e., the number of people who are willing to work is more than necessary, the employers have more options for hiring. Then the labor market is a buyer's market and these workers can work for lower wages. If there are fewer individuals who want to do certain work, the labor market becomes a seller's market and the workers or operators can trade their labor for higher prices.

Furthermore, the fewer the skills needed for a position, the larger the number of people who will be capable of doing it, building a buyer's market. Essentially, the more advanced the skill needed for work, the greater the profit or influence the seller will be able to negotiate. Individuals become educated and more qualified so that they can face the labor market of sellers.

When you start your profession, you are in a buyer's market (unless you have a rare talent) simply because you lack knowledge. As your profession continues, you will gain more diverse experiences and skills, plus you can sell your work in more than one vendor market. You can switch professions or your work at any time, although you should do so to your satisfaction.

Many people only work because of the wages and select jobs according to the salary. However, work is more than a means of revenue; it also serves as a means of personal, intellectual and political satisfaction. Individual compensation for your work can ultimately define your options, but you need to be informed of the exchange value of these decisions as you gain them.

One's labor market status is reflected in the income that is generated. If you are fresh in your profession, you can assume that you will receive less than you desire. Most people want to get to a position where they do not need to trade their time for a job. We all hope to get to a day to pursue our hobbies and other things that interest us. We can retire if we have other means of revenue, which can be created by saving and selling assets.

Capital markets exist for buyers to buy capital. Companies always need resources or funds, but they have only limited funds that can be used. Lenders and sellers (investors) have many ways in which they can invest their monetary surplus in the assets and stock markets. Therefore, these business models are much more like the markets of the seller. The points below are examples of how you can invest or fund in the credit and capital markets:

- Mortgages
- Purchase of shares
- Buy government bonds

Depending on the economic conditions, the demand for a distinct investment or assets may be linked to a market of sellers or buyers. For instance, the real estate market, the modern art market, the sports souvenir market or the vintage automobile market can be buyer markets if there are more merchants than available customers. In general, there are as many as or more interests for funds as there are supplies. The more resources you have available for sale, the higher your chances of selling them to potential buyers. Also, more consumers will be ready to pay. In the beginning, for most individuals, trading time with a job is the only reasonable source of revenue.

How is income spent?

Expenses are accounted for by resources or objects that are consumed or used in daily life. Expenses are recurring. That is, they arise on a continuous basis because of the channels through which payments are made: food, shelter, safety, clothing, transport, etc.

A budget deficit occurs when your income is lower than your expenses and you have limited resources—i.e., little money to fund your desires or needs. A budget shortfall is neither sustainable nor economically viable. The best option is therefore to avoid a financial budget deficit. The means to achieve this, i.e., to eradicate the budget deficit are to increase your income, reduce your expenses or get loans to solve the problem. Obtaining loans to solve the problem can be the smoothest and fastest way to go, but it is only a short-term solution, as you will soon need to pay off the loan. With an additional interest rate on the loan, you know quite well that you do not have the funds to repay it in terms of an increased income.

Revenue can also rise. In such a case, borrowing money to cover a shortage will not deepen it or aggravate it. Some of the better options are to improve your income, cut costs or do both.

There is a budget surplus if your income exceeds the costs incurred for a certain period of time. It is a sustainable situation and therefore financially viable. You can now reduce your income by working less, which is good for your health. There are two ways to do more—save or spend. If you spend (consumption), the excess is gone, but you can appreciate it.

The alternative is to save your money in a piggy bank for future use. However, it is more profitable for you to invest in one of these methods: deposit it into the bank, exchange it for an investment scheme such as shares or real estate, or lend it to someone who will grow your portfolio. By using savings in this way, you will sell your surplus capital to the capital market and therefore increase your cash. Here is a list of ways to register:

1. Deposit your money into a savings account in the bank
2. Contribute to a retirement bank account
3. Purchase a certificate of deposit (CD)
4. Purchase a public savings bank
5. Deposit your money into a money exchange account

Opportunity and diminished costs

Opportunities and sunk costs are hidden costs that influence financial decision-making. In addition to spending, other major types of costs that affect your financial life are opportunity costs and sunk costs.

Assume you can buy either a new dress or shoes, but you don't have the money to buy both. If you purchase the dress, you cannot buy the shoes. Not getting the shoes is an opportunity cost of buying the dress; it is the cost of placing one desire over another.

In private finance, there is always an opportunity value. You must always decide where you get more advantage than the cost. Therefore, the opportunity costs must always be smaller than the profits from the trade. You bought the dress rather than the shoes because you concluded that the dress would be more beneficial than the price of not possessing the shoes. You assumed that your opportunity costs would be lower than your profit.

Opportunity values affect both financial decisions and consumer decisions about personal finance. It's as if you borrow or pay in cash because the payment with savings or cash seems to be free of charge. However, the use of your funds has an opportunity cost.

You will lose cash and any interest you had in your gains. That is when you want money for something like an emergency or a better option, and the funds you need are no longer there for you. Then there is a trend toward financing the loan at a price. After making decisions, sellers and buyers have opportunity costs. Sometimes they have regrets, especially when there is a disappointing return. Sometimes regret can prevent us from seeing sunken costs.

The costs we have incurred are the costs we have already spent. Regardless of how much of the resources we used in the trade are left, there is obviously no way we can get it back. By definition, decisions are made only for the future, not for the past. The business transaction is over, so it is better for you to realize that the money is gone. This attitude can help you make good choices because you will not be emotional.

For instance, the cash you used on your dress would be considered as limited value. Imagine if you have an important event in the next few days. Now it becomes obvious that you need the shoes too, and the cash to pay for them is gone and cannot be recovered. Therefore, you cannot buy the shoes. If you want these shoes, you need to find another way to get them.

Opportunity costs are not obvious. It's not like the daily rates. In most cases, people concentrate on what they are getting from trade and not on something they do not get in exchange. In essence, we ignore the lost opportunities. It is a joyous aspect that is embodied in human beings, although it can be a major weakness if we structure our strategic decisions regarding planning and financial management. It is human nature to concentrate mainly on sunken costs, while knowing that the past cannot be changed. The ability to recognize sunken costs is critical to making good business and financial decisions.

Chapter 9: Assets, Debt and Income

Assets

As mentioned previously, an asset is an element of economic significance that can be exchanged for money. Assets are the resources (including property or capital) that can be used to generate revenue, reduce costs and store value. Examples of tangible assets (materials) include:

- Cars
- Toy collections
- Savings accounts
- Stock shares
- Money exchange accounts
- Houses
- Forty acres of agricultural land

One way to save wealth and probably also generate revenue is to sell the surplus capital on the capital market. The asset becomes your investment or the use of your cash. For example, some ventures are more marketable than others. You could market your car faster and easier than you could sell your home. An asset is used only to store wealth when it has a certain liquidity or market value. This means that it can still be used or is valuable for another person. Before investing, you must consider the liquidity of this asset so you can easily sell your assets and restore your equity. Otherwise, this fortune is obviously not an investment. It is a simple possession to bring good fortune, but does not help you save wealth. Assets can be used to create income, save wealth and diminish later spending.

Assets can store wealth

When an asset is sold, there is goodwill if the venture has more value in resale than it originally acquired. This means the asset has not just saved wealth but has also contributed to the increase. Of course, it can also be different; the asset can fall in value during your ownership and be worth less than when you bought it, so selling would create a loss. The best asset is that which grows in value—generates a capital accumulation—during its period of investment.

Assets can generate revenue

There are assets that can create income and even help save wealth. A investment in a duplex house, for example, saves assets and generates rental income. Some shareholders are more worried about raising the value of assets than revenue. For instance, a share in a company may create a dividend. The dividend is the portion of the company's profit returned to shareholders as a return on their investment. However, shareholders can decide that the company retains all profits instead of paying dividends. The value of the company and the value of its shares increase when the shareholders invest their profits into the business. This increase in the value of the company and the value of the share would also increase the wealth of investors. In addition, capital earnings are charged differently through capital gains, making profits more relevant than rising incomes for some shareholders.

In other words, investors are more concerned about the regular revenue from their assets. For instance, retired people who no longer receive income from work can depend on properties to generate income to offset survival costs. Retirees are usually more concerned with prosperity than with income generation.

Assets can reduce costs

There are also assets that reduce current expenditures. When buying and using, some assets may be more affordable than the cost of other alternatives. For instance, buying and driving a car to work can be less expensive than the cost of using public transport or renting a car in many cases. In general, the car does not increase in its value and cannot save wealth. Its only purpose is to limit future spending.

There are also assets that save wealth and even reduce future spending. When you buy a house, for example, you save the cost of renting. If you live there and save money that would have been used for a rental home, the real estate can increase in its value. This leads to an increase in wealth when you decide to sell the house.

The increase in the value of the house depends on the real estate markets and the demand for housing at the time you decide to sell. However, a home will usually have potential market wealth and reduce your future living expenses. Our decision to invest in an asset depends primarily on our faith in its capability to increase or save wealth, reduce costs or generate income. Typically, an asset will save and improve property, increase revenue, reduce spending or simply increase revenue without reducing spending. If this is not the case, there is no need to acquire this asset because it will not serve as an opportunity to leverage productive liquidity.

Therefore, to gain benefit as an investment, an asset needs to generate income, save wealth or reduce costs. Regardless of the kind of investment chosen, it is much more profitable to invest in assets as opposed to selling capital or labor. The sale of an asset may occur and cause capital accumulation or loss of capital, while the sale of the capital is equivalent to trading on the capital market or the sales market. The sale of capital can take place only if a budgetary surplus of revenue exists above the expenditure.

Debt and capital

The acquisition (or indebtedness) of capital facilitates the investment without the initial presence of capital. If you use other people's money to finance your investment, you have the ability to use property before you own it, provided that the repayment of the asset in the future can adequately cover its costs.

There is no cost for the fair loan. However, the asset must maintain and increase wealth, increase revenue and/or reduce costs sufficiently to balance costs. That is, the asset must be sufficiently productive to compensate for the price of financing (the price of borrowed capital to acquire the asset).

The return of the capital purchase is capital, while the borrowed capital is the debt. Both types of financing capital have values and interests. Once you borrow or buy capital, you become a buyer on the money market.

Costs of debt and equity

You can purchase a property from different investors in exchange for a stake or participation. Participation in real estate or equity represents your entitlement to future income or future revenue. If the investment is fruitful, (because of extra revenue or diminishing costs) the shareholder or the owner benefits depending on the proportion of the assets held. When the asset loses its significance, the owner takes a share of the loss according to the portion of the property owned. The profit from the investment is the cost of capital.

A loan is the rent of another person's funds for a period, and the outcome is debt. During this time, the rent or dividend is paid, which represents a debt cost. When this period expires, each principal (the principal) must be repaid. The investment gain must be sufficient to satisfy the interest of the capital and capital growth must be sufficient to reduce the initial capital. The person who borrowed is held responsible for paying back the loan, which creates a liability.

In turn, the price of ownership is paid only if there happens to be a rise in wealth or income, and even then it can be postponed. There is a direct impact on expenditure and income when the liquidity loan (debt) is acquired.

Use of debt and investment

Technically, debt is a way to acquire an investment or a property that you do not have the financial ability to acquire outright. If the asset tends to achieve sufficient performance (i.e. increase in value, increase in income or reduction in costs) to cover the additional costs, the debt may be worthwhile. However, if the debt constitutes additional costs without sufficient additional benefits, it cannot be useful. The risk is that although the expenses are known in advance, the interest payments are not. This debt risk to create more debt is an important factor that must be assessed. Consider the typical example from the events that occurred near the end of 2008, when homeowners began losing the benefit of their respective homes because of falling house prices. Some homeowners had the misfortune of having debts that were larger than their homes' resale value. They knew the cost ahead of time, but they never predicted a decrease in the value of their houses. They did not know the consequences of borrowing based on the assumption of rising house prices.

Debts can also be utilized to overcome the budget deficit (surplus of expenditure relative to income). However, in the longer term, the value of debt can double the costs that were previously too large. If the income cannot be increased, more debt will only worsen the deficit.

Mortgage value

The cost of the debt implies the use of the assets sooner rather than later, which allows for financing the loan. For example, people need to buy an apartment as soon as they start having children. This may be because they want toilets, bedrooms and perhaps a playground. Young adults as potential buyers have not necessarily saved enough to purchase the house directly, so to balance the difference they choose to borrow. However, this means that they will pay interest on the loan for the duration of their mortgage.

You have the alternative of renting a living space. In cases in which the rent for a moderate home is higher than the debt repayment for a mortgage, use a mortgage to purchase a house. The rooms, bathrooms and playgrounds that a house has are useful for children while they are young and live in an apartment. Waiting until you have saved sufficiently to buy a house could mean you are much older and having children could be more difficult.

Another typical instance of the value of a debt is the use of a mortgage to finance education. Education is useful because it can be appreciated over a period. One advantage is an improvement in the potential for gains in earnings and wages. The demand for qualified personnel is much higher than for illiterate or short-skilled workers. As a result, education creates a number of relevant and thus more expensive workers.

It is useful to maximize the value by receiving training as quickly as possible so that you can enjoy the maximum time to work at a higher salary. It is even logical to finance an education before you begin working because your costs of attending school—and in this case, the "wasted" salary of not working—are lower. Without savings to fund your studies, you will usually borrow. Debt allows you to gain the benefit of education to increase your income, and from this you will be able to repay the debts.

Another option would be to continue working and saving until you can afford to acquire an education. However, you will earn less than you would if you were qualified. Then, when you start work as a qualified person, you have less time to make a higher rate of wages. Waiting to go to college diminishes the value or usefulness of your education during your life.

In the case of financing, the assets acquired in equity are equal to the holding and also the profits or losses they incur, while the assets granted by loans and the creation of a debt constitute a financial responsibility that must be fulfilled.

Income and risks

The concept of personal finances does not involve only getting what you need; it also includes the protection of what you have. The way to acquire assets is to generate surplus funds. A surplus of capital requires you to have an income higher than your expenditure. As one is dependent on revenue to finance life expenses, it is important to protect one's income. One process protects income through the diversification of risks.

Putting all eggs into a single basket is like sitting in a mine waiting for the explosion to go off at any time. If something should happen to this basket, all your eggs will be gone! However, if you drop eggs into several baskets and you lose one of those baskets, you've only lost a fraction of the total income you have. This process of putting eggs into more than one basket is called diversification. However, diversifying your eggs across many baskets but putting them in the same environment still exposes them to the same risk that is faced by the person who has all eggs in one basket. Therefore, an effective approach to diversification is to place many eggs in many baskets and place baskets in different places so that they are not in the same economic environment.

Diversification is most often applied in investment portfolios, but the diversification of income sources uses the same logical reasoning. If the income streams are diversified in number and in kind, and a source of revenue is no longer productive, others can still be working.

Doing business with only one customer (or working for only one employer) presents more risks in generating income compared to the sale of goods or services to more than one customer. As a supplier of workers or employees, it is almost impossible to deal with more than one organization. One company could be physically demanding, take a long time to pay and pose a serious risk to your livelihood. The supply of jobs in the market also implies that employers are still very much reliant on the labor market, even though negative parts of the economic cycle (such as a recession) can quickly change the flow of things.

Consider the example of Frank, who works as a teacher. He teaches private students at night, paints houses in the summer, and purchases and markets sports equipment on the web. If Frank was dismissed from his teaching job, he would lose his salary, but he could still earn income through tutoring, painting houses and trading sports equipment on the Internet.

Furthermore, if you are investing in a single asset, you are in danger of falling into the same situation. Diversification of investments means you depend on trading on the resources markets, which could also suffer with unfortunate economic circumstances. For example, Agnes works as an economic analyst and has a retail clothing business with an online delivery account. By chance, she loses her job as an analyst but still has her retail clothes business, which she could probably expand. In this case, she had a secondary asset to fall back on, which gave her enough time to assess and try other options without fear or pressure. A reliable way to diversify is to make sure that some or all your investments are not in the same category, so if something happens, all your income sources will not be affected at the same time. Thus, selling or working in numerous markets prevents you from being completely exposed to the risks that are associated with each of them.

To diversify, you need capital for trading, which is explained in the quote from Adam Smith: "It demands money to make money." The idea is not to have surplus money as the richest billionaire in the world, but to have a budget surplus that is created by living a lifestyle in which your income is always more than your expenses. Such people realize that someone who spends frivolously would eventually go into debt while a sensitive person who accepts the minimalist lifestyle would find it easy to have a budget surplus. Therefore, diversification becomes a feasible option and a way of happiness only for minimalists.

Chapter 10: Budgeting

It is often easier to imagine the value of achieving a goal than trying to achieve that goal. This is a typical situation for people who engage in self-improvement plans for themselves. When they make decisions, there is a lot of determination, effort and dedication. However, the planning is often not well thought-out and people do not know the steps they need to take to get the results they want.

Considering finances, Pro forma financial statements postulate reports that reflect changes in the actual financial statements. They give an overview of the possible results of financial decisions that were made during a time period. They can also be used as tools for planning actions that need to be taken to achieve specific financial results.

When projected in the form of a budget (which represents a projection of the financial conditions and stages of the plan), the figures represent estimates that come from previous actual data. If the estimates do not match the actual data after time has passed, the failures or achievements can be used to come up with future strategies.

Budgets are usually created with a fixed goal in mind: increase savings, reduce living costs or save for a specific purpose such as retirement, education or housing. Although items on the budget can draw attention to specific needs, it is actually meant to outline specifics as to how specific goals can be achieved. In other words, the budget document is more an action document than a reflection of what you have in mind.

Also, a budget must be dynamic because there are always contingencies and unexpected events. Real life will affect how your planned budget is spent. While the annual accounts show your past numbers (that is, they reveal everything that has already happened and is "sunk"), budgets are meant to reflect current and projected numbers. Therefore, a budget should never be simply followed, but should be constantly reviewed and revised so it takes into account new issues that are constantly emerging.

Budgeting process

The budgeting process is an inexhaustible loop, as is the broader financial planning process. The steps include:

- Objective setting and data collection
- Creating expectations and comparing objectives with data
- Creating the budget
- Monitoring the actual result and performing variance analysis
- Budgeting and adapting to new objectives
- Redefining the goals

A summary of your current financial accounts and your own ideas of how you can live should show immediate and long-term goals. This can also mean you have new options that you mean want to explore. For instance, an immediate goal might be to find the least expensive house. You might want to rent a place for cheap temporarily even though you have plans to buy a property of your own in the long run. The long-term objective may require you to implement a provision plan for obtaining a mortgage.

The act of writing a statement can be enlightening. With a budget, your predictions will be realistic. Your assumptions can change according to your past behavior, which is based on the exact accounts you accumulated. You can use private investment software to keep these records; otherwise, a detailed check of your personal check book and asset instructions will be required to get this information. Annual financial records are valuable reports that are required to draw up a statement.

After realizing realistic expectations based on historic performance and current situations, you should always compare your future goals with your own expectations. For instance, you might find that you need to make bigger sacrifices, or you need to change your attitude, or maybe your aims are not achievable or maybe you can even go one step further to aim at a higher goal.

Whether you end up with serious disappointment or ambitious happiness, the budgeting process is about unifying your financial actualities with your financial goals. How you finance your life will directly impact your personal life. Therefore, budgeting is a way of approaching life on a day to day basis. It can be hard to ignore the financial sacrifices related to your goals, but the more efficient you are in taking the right steps, the more you'll achieve your goals.

A budget is a guess of how it should work. However, there will always be uncertainty. If the original results are more pleasant than what is required or if your income is more than your expenditure, expectations can become better. If the outcomes are worse than anticipated or if the income is reduced, the subsequent budget and current lifestyle options need to be revised to reflect this situation.

To avoid unwanted budget changes, you must be cautious in your own personal expectations to increase the likelihood that your original predictions will be higher than expected. Therefore, once you are done estimating, you want to constantly revisit the financial gain or inherent earnings and surpass the inherent expenses and losses.

You must maintain a schedule for your budget estimating process: yearly, monthly or weekly. This timing can change based on an increase in financial activity or the level of control you want to have on your budget. You should evaluate your performance at least once a year. However, you will have to manage a lot of information on a daily basis. The more income and expenditures you have, the more your budget should be reviewed. Your accounts should be systematically monitored and you should not be flooded with too much information. On the other hand, you need to decide when you will sit down and "report" significant results. You want to choose a review period that aligns with the end of your tax year or financial cycle. The budget process reflects the entire financial preparation process and is meant to help you compare estimated data with actual data. When evaluating, a conservative approach is best because it involves the undervaluation of income and the over-assignment of expenses.

Create a full budget

The first steps that need to be performed include data collection and the creation of a statement. In addition, the arrangement of the statement will help you because you will be able to filter through excess information to get the important information you actually need. A complete budget (i.e. a budget that incorporates all aspects of the monetary life) includes a forecast of current ongoing revenue and expenses as well as one-time expenses. (One-time financial gains or "extraordinary gains" should not be included.) Continuous income would come from earnings, profits or dividends. Current expenses include life costs, credit compensations and conventional savings or property charges. One-time expenses may include money needed for capital developments, such as replacement of your home or to buy other goods such as a refrigerator or a car. These are the purchases that are not made every month. Another characteristic of the recognition of continuous and non-recurring expenditures is that the timing varies for everyone. Current expenditures need to be addressed repeatedly and are therefore considered on short notice, while investment budgets could provide for long-term preparation because they do not need to be visited frequently. Setting different time frames for continuous and non-recurring elements could provide you with different methods for achieving these objectives.

A complete budget is made up of two parts. It has a summary of the operational budget that is used to fulfill short-term objectives (including recurring items) and a long-term capital budget that has non-recurring items.

Budget management: Recurring revenue and expenditure

Revenue and recurring expenses are sometimes the simplest to identify and project because they are systematically ongoing, and also have an immediate impact on our daily lives. An income report shows income and expenses while the income statements show the actual monetary expenditure. Current revenue and expenses are expected to cover short-term lifestyle goals or financial decisions.

Consider a time frame that is reasonable for capturing relevant information. Some revenue and expenditures are repeated sporadically or occasionally. For instance, you might pay your car insurance in two instalments per year. This is an ongoing cost. However, it occurs in only two months of the year. Therefore, you should remember the months so that you can go to corresponding records and review the costs if you need to. In addition, your utility costs can change according to the season and affect your usage bills in other months.

The time period selected for budgeting should be long enough to meet intermittent issues such as continuous and non-recurring items and to make decisions throughout that time. For individual budgets, one month is likely the most typical time frame for a budget plan, as most bills are paid monthly. Nevertheless, it is best to use a whole year of data to deduce an affordable monthly amount because you will see yearly and periodic events that have taken place.

Some items can be repeated but not reliably. Their recurrence or amount is uncertain. Using a cautious approach, you need to accept the highest potential amount of unsafe spending in your statements. However, if the financial gain occurs frequently, the number should be set to the smallest amount that is prudent. If the financial gain is irregular, it would be better to exclude it from your budget (and also from your projects) because you cannot count on it.

Consider the following example. Alan works as a university consultant and a tutor. He paints during the summers and also purchases and sells sports records on the Internet. In 2006, Alan purchased an old house with a fixed-rate mortgage of $200,000 at 5.5%. Every year, he puts $1,000 into his retirement savings account and uses the money for home improvement. He used a car loan to purchase his car. Any remaining money after he has paid his bills is recorded in a market record that gains 3% interest. At the end of 2009, Alan is attempting to propose a budget to take 2010 into account. Since he acquired his house, Alan has kept smart financial records.

Alan has five income sources. Some are consistent, some are not. Also, some are seasonal. His consulting work ensures continuous revenue throughout the year. Painting is seasonal but provides a fairly good source of revenue. However, in 2008 the amount was smaller because Alan fell from a stairway and could not paint for over three months. Tutoring can be an annual means of income but since the college employed an additional consultant in 2008, his workload was reduced. His online business varies from year to year and so offers unpredictable financial gains. In 2009, operations were very profitable, but in 2007, he sold almost nothing. The profit from the business depends on the surplus of the capital exchange account. He would include his painting and consulting income in his budget, but he should be cautious about incorporating his tutoring or online business income.

Alan's issues are stable and easy to predict, with one minor exception. His injury in 2008 raised his medical costs for that year. Fuel and heating costs vary according to the climate and consequently, the price of oil was highly volatile. In 2008, these expenditures were remarkably high. However, it is unlikely that the 2009 capital tax will continue to inflate.

Alan knows that the hiring of a new tutor significantly affected his tutoring income. Alan may have a modest increase in his salary, but he has been informed that the advance payments and deductibles in his medical and dental coverage could go up in 2010. Alan just got a loan for an "almost-new" used car.

With this familiar monetary history, it would be necessary to capture new data that will change expectations. As with any projection, the more knowledge you can use in your forecast, the better.

Individual or minor characteristics of an environment influence our expectations, especially when they change. Factors such as family composition, health, alternative careers and age have major impacts on monetary and objective decisions. If one of these factors should vary, it is expected that its monetary scenario will also vary. Therefore, it is important to keep such factors incorporated in future budget forecasts.

For instance, if you are hoping to extend or reduce the amount spent on your family, you may have to change your way of consuming products and services. If you are planning to change your job or career, your budget may be affected because of a new salary. A change in health conditions could lead to much more (or less) work and thus affect your working income. There are several ways in which individual circumstances improve, and they will cause you to adjust your business expectations, options and aims in life. All of these planned changes should be incorporated into your budget.

Considering macro factors

The macro factors that affect your estimates come from the circumstances of the economy. In general, you want to find out how income and costs are generated because the knowledge will help you make estimates. Income is generated when work or money is sold. The cost of revenue generated relies on the number of goods (or services) sold and their respective costs.

The price of labor relies on the dependent supply and interest of labor, which is reflected in the unemployment rate. The change in liquidity prices relies on the corresponding interest rate and quotation quotas. Interest rates and unemployment rates rely on a dynamic and complex market.

The economy is actually cyclical. If the market enters a phase of consolidation or recession, the labor demand will be low, competition among employees will be high and salaries would not be expected to increase. When unemployment increases, especially when you work in an enterprise that is cyclical within a market, earnings can become unstable or risky for you because your job security goes down. The profit rates become unstable and more complicated to forecast, but tend to be in a phase of contraction, after which they sink into the expansion phase. The budgetary time period is usually short, so the economic factors do not change enough to affect the projections during this short period. However, these economic factors affect the estimates of potential resources that are available.

Expenses are generated as soon as a certain number of products or services are bought. These costs are based on the applicable supply and demand of these products and services as well as on the wider context of price levels in the market. When deflation or a boom influences the price of money (through an increase or decrease), it changes its purchasing power and the real price of spending. Here, too, the budgetary time should be short so that fluctuations in purchasing potential do not have much impact on the budget, even if these variations should not be overlooked. Demand levels change more quickly than earning levels. Therefore, it is entirely plausible to have an increase in costs before an increase in salaries, which reduces the actual purchasing potential of your pay check.

Suppose you have a changeable rate loan, i.e., the type for which the investment rate can be periodically changed. You are subject to the volatility of the interest rates. You should remember this unique macro circumstance when planning your resources.

Macroeconomic determinants are hard to predict because they present complex situations, but information on the current expected financial positions is available both inside and outside the media. A sound financial director or planner must also monitor the economic indicators critically. In your forecasts, you should have a remarkably strong idea of the state of the economy and how it affects you directly by understanding the way your pay check impacts your life costs (e.g., buying food or filling your vehicle with gasoline). History, up-to-date information and the recognition of current and expected macroeconomic circumstances can be used to develop resource forecasts.

Let's consider the previous case study. To predict his income, Alan used his latest information to determine his tutoring and consulting income. He applied the smallest revenue of the past four years for the souvenir business, which is logical because the income is volatile. His paint revenue is less unpredictable, so his calculation is an aggregate, and does not include the year of his injury. Business revenue is based on the present money exchange surplus, which is lowered by the expected rate of interest.

Alan expects that spending in 2009 will remain the same, as prices and the rate of consumption will not change. However, he needs to modify the medical and dental insurance, as well as his car payments. Alan understands that the more experience and intelligence he brings to his budget, the more realistic and beneficial his estimates will be.

Capital budget

Income that remains after the payment of life expenses and liabilities or free money is available for capital or investment. Fund expenses are often part of a long-term strategy to build up a wealth of assets. Investments can also be part of a longer-term idea of constructing an asset or accomplishing a specific aim, such as financing education.

Long-term forecasts are based on the expected changes in the macro circumstances that affect goals. The expansion or reduction of the family can create new austerity measures or a variation in home needs that change the asset situation (e.g., acquiring or selling a house).

Some modifications will "remove" a specific goal. A person who has completed college, for instance, has "removed" the education financial requirement. Some changes undermine the need for a goal, such as health deterioration that reduces the risk of a poor retirement. Because personal factors vary, you should re-evaluate your long-term goals and investment portfolio because the amount of investment funds may vary accordingly.

Although many private factors are expected over the long term (e.g., people age and have no children), the wider economic factors over the same period are very difficult to forecast. Will the market rise or fall when you retire? Will there be deflation or inflation? When you are meeting your targets, it will be more difficult to anticipate these factors, and they might be less important to your immediate interests. As you meet your goals, macroeconomic circumstances will become more relevant in assessing your performance.

As long-term plans occur over time, you must use the correlation between value and time to calculate investment expenditures and successful achievements. Long-term goals are best achieved through a series of consistent steps. For example, a savings goal should be achieved by submitting a series of consistent deposits into your account. These routine deposits will eventually form an annuity. Knowing how long an annuity exists and the savings you accumulate will allow you to convert your account statement (the current value of the pension) inside your savings account to a future value amount. You can then measure the impact of your deposits that are going in the account. After evaluation, the amounts can be tailored to maximize your personal cash flow so you know exactly how much you should be saving. You can likewise see if your goal is too simple or too complex. You can then either change the time period or the rate of payments to adjust as necessary.

An investment can be a one-time expenditure, such as a new home. An investment can also be an action toward a long-term goal, as well as a yearly savings account. This objective should be judged with each fund and the "stages" of investment activity should be checked according to your set time intervals.

Consider the previous case study. Alan's 2010 budget includes a reduction in revenue and income and an increase in the cost of living, which leaves little free money for investment. He knows his house needs a new roof (which is estimated at $15,000). He hopes it will happen in the year 2010. Nevertheless, this investment would cause a different net cash stream to come into his account from the money market. Alan's budget shows his current preferences for life in the short term (expected revenue and spending) and improvements that are required to meet his longer-term goals (developing the property and savings) without getting adjustments and options. What should these changes and decisions be? This is the question that needs to be answered.

Treasury/Cash budget

If the payment streams are not periodic, that is, if they are influenced by seasonality or a different occurrence rate than the budget time rate, taking a closer look at the bank can be valuable. Although the cash flow may be sufficient to support the annual expenditure, there could be temporary hiccups. Income-related cash flows can be less common than cash streams related to costs, for instance, or they can be periodic, while spending is more general. Most expenses must be financed on a regular basis. Moreover, if certain payment flows of revenue happen at limited times, or only periodically, there is a risk of that there will be a lack of money in a particular month. Time is necessary for all cash flows.

An excellent management tool is a list of capital resources, because it shows the resources in detail every 30 days. Abnormal cash streams can be found in the various months in which they occur so that you can see the impact of cash flows more directly.

In our case study, Alan's initial annual estimates support his spending on investments, especially the repairing of the roof of his house. In fact, his cash flow will increase to around $6,870. If he must make investment expenditures this year, he can fund them with a credit line (a loan by which one borrows money) if necessary to pay up to a specific point.

The capital budget presents a more specific and slightly more complex tale. Because of Alan's annual income, if he has a fixed cap in the month of May, he has to borrow $10,525 in May. Then he would pay this balance by October if he had to re-emphasize the payment of his property tax. At the end of the year, his prominent debt may be slightly higher than originally stated, with a final excess of $6,887. However, all his interest expenses would be a little less (just $221) because the loan surplus and hence the cost of profit will be lower in some of the time periods.

The monthly budget tells a more distinctive story than the yearly budget because of the recurring nature of Alan's income. Given the fact that he is preparing investment payments before he starts generating paint income, he must rent more and take more risks than expected.

The capital budget can present both risks and corrections that may not remain obvious. In Alan's case, it is very likely that investment spending cannot be funded without another source of funds such as a credit facility. He should pay credit on this new loan and incur additional costs. This effort would be symmetrical to the borrowed money and the period for which it was borrowed. In Alan's original plan, investment spending took place in the month of May, and Alan would have received loans of approximately $10,525 with which he could pay credit for the following seven months of that year. The delay in spending on investments until October would cost him less. However, he has to lend less and pay interest in less than a few months. If he can invest by October, he would cause the capital market account to increase its value (Alan's yearly revenue would be deposited in the summertime), which would fund more investment funds. He can choose to borrow less money and finish the year with around $6,557, so his interest expense would be just $123 because he has fewer loans and because he can push up loans to October. Then the interest is applied for just three months of the year.

Synchronization is important for cash flow because you need to make money before you can say it's time to spend it, although monetary values are affected by time. It is always advisable to have money and to hang on to it even longer. A capital budget presents an extremely comprehensive view of these time issues and cash management possibilities that you may have overlooked.

Other functional budgets

A streamlined budget could be an estimate that forecasts a certain facet of your investments such as cash flow. Other forms of concentrated resources specify a specific facet or a financial goal. Ultimately, a special budget exists in the overall budget, as this could be part of your overall financial activity. This always reflects a specific activity with additional details, including the impact of ownership and maintenance of a selected asset or a selected activity. Generate resources for this asset or activity by separating your revenue and expenses from your entire accounts. It is conceivable that you could design a specific budget as long as you can determine and separate your financial goals from the others in your life. However, you must track a one activity at a given time to fully reap the benefits of budgeting.

Suppose you want to hike on the weekends as a leisure activity. You can try it for at least 24 months and then decide whether you wish to proceed. Apart from evaluating the enjoyment it offers you, you must also be able to evaluate its impact on your investments. Usually, the weekend hiker needs special clothing and equipment while traveling to a campground or hiking on trails. Depending on what kind of hiker the person is, food and a booking at a hotel may be required. The point is that capital investments and recurring costs accumulate when it comes to leisure activities. You may need to generate different income streams to manage this new leisure activity and evaluate whether the cost is worth the self-fulfilment or enjoyment that it brings to your life.

There are other budgets that can be made to include different resources. The types of resources in a household budget include activities (income, profits, losses and expenses) that have at least some tax implications. A tax budget could be worth planning or forecasting to assess how much wealth will be given to the government. This assessment would be done on revenue from self-employment, a portfolio of equities, property, a single gift of substantial wealth or the establishment of a property portfolio.

While it makes sense to separate and recognize the impact of another activity or work toward a different goal, this goal or activity is ultimately only a portion of your comprehensive financial being. Specific budgets should only be a fraction of your overall financial wealth as they are not meant to be excessive.

Budget changes

The budgetary deviation happens when your day-to-day activities deviate from your budgetary projections. Given the fact that your expectations are based on your knowledge of micro and macroeconomy, your financial history and new knowledge may mean that your estimates are no longer accurate, as one or probably more of these factors could have fluctuated suddenly. If your estimation is incorrect, you may have omitted or neglected a factor. Once you understand what's missing, you can change it. When one or more of these factors suddenly changes, you will have to do a reanalysis to tweak things as they need to be tweaked. At least, the changes will inform you that you need to improve your resources or look for other options of management.

If you possess resources, your business life will generally be easy. Given that the current data will replace the forecast data to date, you need to watch the funds for your original projects so you can see significant deviations or variations from the anticipated results in those resources. The interpretation and knowledge of variations and new information is needed to adapt their current behaviour and allow them to realistically re-evaluate their goals.

The earlier you spot a budget difference, the sooner you can examine it and correct it if necessary. The sooner you fix the gap, the less it will cost. For example, you may have had minor problems, so you must build a way to support your achievement of that goal. You have come up with a scenario, and complete data is necessary to understand the impact on your forecast. In your initial budget, you assumed you had a load to get gas in your vehicle, which you calculated by determining the distance you were driving and the current gas price. You look at your account and you discover that the cost of gas has increased. That means you:

- Spend less on other expenses, so your total cost remains in the range.
- Reduce your fuel costs by driving less and growing your income to cover the largest expenses.
- Build your revenue to increase spending.

Meanwhile, in the short term, tracking your gas costs tells you how to improve your management by doing more with less expensive transportation choices. Although this is unsustainable in the long run, you can re-order your other options to solve this problem. Maybe you need a more economic vehicle, for instance, or need to change your lifestyle to require more limited driving. The viability and quality of your decisions depend on the flexibility of the different budget forecasts. However, if you aren't careful and do not verify your estimates against the actual results as they unfold, there is a possibility you will not know what changes are necessary. This could also mean that you might miss an unexpected budget deficit if you are not paying attention.

Let's suppose that by reviewing during that time period, you found a substantial budget variance, so you need to examine what issues it has created to sort it out correctly.

- Revenue comes from the exchange of effort or liquidity (profit or bonuses).
- Another amount of cash or labor was traded at the same price. (For example, it had less housing deals than normal, but insisted its prices were the same.)
- The expected volume of work or liquidity was less than expected.

- A certain amount of liquidity or labor was exchanged at a different price (e.g., fewer contracts and less invoiced than expected.)
- Investments from the use of assets or services were at a cost that was more than planned.
- A different amount was used compared to the usual amount (e.g., not as much gas).
- Another quantity has been used at a different rate. (For example, you used a smaller vehicle which uses cheaper gas and can be purchased at a lower price.)

It is good to isolate the causes of variance because the various cases require a remedy and can also create different possibilities. For instance, if gas costs have risen, is it because you are driving farther distances or because the gas price has increased? You cannot adjust the gas price, but you can check the distance you travel. Cause isolation enables you to recognize practical benefits. In this instance, if the variation is too expensive, you need to approach it in some other way.

If income falls, will you say this happens as a result of your decreasing hourly salary or a reduction in the number of hours worked? Nevertheless, your salary has decreased, so you should attempt to improve it by bargaining with your employer or looking for new work with a higher salary. Your success depends on the demands of the business and its value to others.

While you work shorter hours, your company may give you a smaller job. Therefore, the problem is with your business; you want to renegotiate your position or find a new one. However, if your organization is purchasing less work because of a lower labor market demand, this can affect your industry and your search for a new job.

Recognizing why you deviate from your plan is important so you can identify remedies and options. Realizing these problems in the setting of micro and macro factors will make your options more manageable.

In the previous example, how will Alan examine the statement changes he notices? He has selected a few educated customers who have entrusted themselves to Alan's consultancy and who will be invoiced in June. This new knowledge can be applied to change his income. His commercial contacts worked well; the sales volume has not improved, but the souvenir business appears to have done well, and the increased income is more than enough. The buy and selling of souvenirs is cyclical because business growth and increased income levels are improving this business. Given the low values in this market and the reality that there was no improvement in sales volumes, Alan won't need to adjust the income for the future period. Business valuations have increased, so Alan can use the macroeconomic news to change the expected interest rate.

The unique difference is the issue of Alan's decision to reduce his travel and production resources this year (i.e., abandon his leave) to compensate for the cost of the home. Including these changes means that Alan will be able to avoid new debts and still maintain investment spending on his home. The forecasts need ongoing follow-up. Unusual increases are attributable to the efforts of Alan (reduced entertainment spending, holiday rebates and the new tutoring clients). However, Alan also sees effects from macroeconomic factors that have developed to his satisfaction (rising interest rates, rising prices of souvenirs), and these factors could return to their loss. He has been trying to remain cautious about the future, although he should proceed to monitor the situation closely, especially if he intends to make comparatively large capital expenditures in October. It's seldom that a change cannot be "improved" or pushed out of its control due to a microeconomic or macroeconomic circumstance. In this case, he needs to change his expectations. He may need to change the forecast results and maybe also his final goals.

Variations are also measurements of the efficiency of your forecasts. By using forecasting, you increase your appraisals and budgeting experience. The unforeseen always happens, so the more experience you get, the more accurate and valuable the budgeting process becomes.

Budgets, financial statements and decisions

Regardless of the variety of resources it produces, the budget method is a facet of monetary design and a tool for the creation of better financial choices. Alternative ways include business reports, risk assessments and the present cost of capital, macroeconomic forecasts and microeconomic or personal factors. The benefit of these devices is that they provide a clearer reading of "everything" and "everything is possible." They present your current scenario and also your options in a broader context so that you can trust your forecasts more. In addition, they will help you get to where you want to be.

Alan should decide whether he wants a new home. Suppose the building requires a replacement roof. He just needs to decide if he should fund it or not. An analysis of Alan's budget deviations showed that he could actually get the cap including the profits toward his capital business record. That implies his purpose is more feasible (and cheaper) compared to his original budget. The positive result is attributable to attempts to improve revenue and reduce costs and overall economic changes. As a result, Alan can shift his attention to his long-term goal of increasing his assets. He can extend his retirement with securities in his pension plan and can also advance more money on his house, including an extension on his home.

Because Alan finances the cap with profits from his capital market account, he can withdraw new debts and thereby increase his income. He loses investment interest from his cash business statement (which is negligible because it accounts for only 0.09% of his total income). However, his sales revenue and tutoring can compensate for the loss. Alan's income will not be affected by the home. His fund's cash flow record, therefore, shows a constant cash flow, excessive costs and the advantage of reservations.

Alan can support this development in the value of the asset. His credit order does not change significantly (the value will change only from one good to another), but the capital exchange account earns what the house appears not to, even though there might be a profit if the house is assigned in the future.

Presently, the investment interest is irrelevant. However, as this appears to be a time of increasing interest valuations, the possible cost of lost interest revenue could be substantial assuming that the balance of this account was allowed to grow.

Also, Alan will transfer the value of a highly commercial capital exchange account to a house that will reduce his total liquidity. For the future, this cash loss could lead to further opening costs that could reduce his alternatives. Alan's stock will be almost exhausted by the cover. Therefore, future investment expenditures can be financed by the deficit. If profit rates grow, this will make the financing of future investment expenses more costly, causing Alan to delay or eliminate them.

Despite the fact that Alan also has solid liquidity in his income (his salary check, which can compensate for the damage), if he can still generate an open cash progress to add more to his savings, he can restore his capital market statement and liquidity. Without committing himself, Alan is more capable of facing the possibility of exhausting his current cash and depending on his interest to relaunch it.

These costs of opening the liquidity loss and gain revenue will be lower than the expenses of the new debt and the new investment spending. That is because the investment rates on advances are continually greater than the interest rates on the savings. Banks always charge more than they reward for cash. This spread, or the difference between these two rates, is the advantage of the bank. Therefore, the price of the bank when buying money is always less than the value it sells. The additional risk and liability of new debts can together generate opportunity costs and make it harder to finance future investment spending. As a result, the financing of investments including an asset is both immediate and less costly in the expectation that they have fewer additional obligations and possibilities, fewer opening costs and less chance.

The budgetary and monetary accounts allow Alan to predict the consequences of this fiscal determination in the broader context of his current economic scenario and his final financial targets. His perception of opening costs, cash, the present value of money, and individual and macroeconomic factors helps Alan assess his decisions and outcomes. Alan can also use this option to resolve any upcoming issues and decisions.

Commercial planning is an ongoing process of financial decision-making. The annual accounts are meant to summarize current circumstances and calculate the final results. The analysis of the annual reports and the analysis of the budgetary deviation are methods for assessing the consequences of decisions. Economic factors and personal factors, as well as their relationship over time (uncertainty and value), influence decisions because of how the work dynamics affect the results.

The ongoing process of making financial decisions is called financial planning. Although the ways used to predict results are related to budgeting, the annual accounts deal with the summary of the current circumstances. The analysis of the financial situation and deviation are methods for assessing the impact of decisions. Factors that affect these options are: economic and personal factors, risk, time and value.

Chapter 11: Individual Financial Planning

Identification of the starting point

We are stuck on the way or at the beginning. For some people, starting can be one of the most difficult phases. You can start by listing your forecasts and then progressing to defining your priorities. The idea is to take small, incremental steps that help you create plans because we are not mentally competent to take in the immensity of everything. If you have an excellent financial plan, divide it into smaller steps and then run it in small increments as long as it is relatively simple and you aren't embarrassed in doing so. Taking action is especially useful for fighting chronic procrastination.

Be determined (take the pledge)

Financial planning begins with a personal or corporate decision to change the way in which finances are handled. This is often born of the desire to achieve financial stability. This need should also be communicated to one's spouse and other important family members who may influence the success or failure of decisions.

People should try to keep these commitments firmly in mind when they see advertising campaigns pointing to different consumer goods. Buying more things will only increase spending. With the massive number of catchy ads and attractive promotions, it is important that those who choose to make informed financial decisions are protected from their influence.

If one is committed to change, an individual or a family must define their responsibilities and structures. A person may require the services of a financial advisor, an accountant or a portfolio manager to investigate available sources of income and viable investment options. For a family, while all members must be aware of the general financial situation, choosing a person to maintain the daily financial responsibilities is a great way to keep up with things.

The first step in designing your personal finances is to decide to respect the changes you make. You must be mentally prepared to respect your budget. This may be a small step, but let me assure you, it is as important as any other step you take to improve your financial structure. It's easy to decide to curb impulses, but when you go to the mall with a friend and see a bright, attractive item that makes your mouth water, how do you react? Do you buy it impulsively or do you stick with your current budget? Mental preparation is as important as any other measure. Refuse to move when you are in a hurry to spend money on items that are not included in your budget. Do not ignore this step.

Assessment of the current financial situation

Know your financial goals. If you do not have any at the moment, it is time to define them clearly and precisely. Would you like to be financially independent? When do you want to be? When would you like to retire? How much money do you want? Would you like to retire sooner or later? You must have as much clarity as possible when you do this.

It is also a good time to make financial resources available. What options are available at short notice and what are your options in the long term? More importantly, look for options that can serve you in both the short term and the future. After this process, list each of your assets. Also highlight your tasks and write them down in detail. Include all taxes on assets, deferred tax assets, corporate bonds, mortgages, shares, loans and anything else that has an impact on your finances and allows you to assess your good and bad debt. Because of this exercise, it will be easier to determine whether your net worth is increasing or decreasing.

Next, consider your risk including the amount of risk you can take on without losing your head when you decide to invest. Know whether you are a cautious, aggressive or a moderate investor by making your money work for you. This allows you to identify the future investments you should or should not carry out.

The assessment of your current financial situation is not limited or fixed in the balance sheet. A complete evaluation is required. This will build your ability to plan and manage financial products while still giving you the financial knowledge you need.

A quick financial measure is the net worth of an individual. It is a balance between the assets and liabilities a person has. Are your net assets increasing in relation to other years? What is the relationship between income and debt?

The assets include shares and bonds; amounts in savings banks, money market funds, pension funds and retirement accounts. You also want to include current market values of properties belonging to special collections, such as art, collectors' items and other luxury items.

Debt represents liabilities on the balance sheet. The debt profile of a person also provides an indicator of the person's current financial situation. There are many reasons to borrow and a variety of options for doing so. Some debts are inevitable, like school loans and mortgages. This is why many young people start their working lives with debt. Other debts include automobile loans, home improvement loans, leases and credit card loans. However, good financial management will lead to a gradual reduction in past debt and little to no new debt. People with poor financial management tend to have increasing short-term and long-term debt and tend to use expensive credit methods.

Are there short-term and long-term savings? This is an important indicator for planning. Some short-term needs you can plan and save for include vacations and additional training. The ability to meet these needs provides an indicator of the financial situation of an individual. A savings account, which can support three to six months of normal spending if current income falls, is recommended. Long-term savings—for example, in the field of old-age provision—reflect financial management. For example, do you make any contributions, random contributions or maximum contributions to retirement accounts? The ability to produce consistent contributions suggests sound budgetary management.

The assessment of the current financial situation also includes the examination of the investment options a person uses. Is it necessary to rebalance the investment portfolio? Can investment costs be reduced by changing consultants and portfolio managers?

Elimination of financial disruption

A financial burden is when you have too many invoices because you buy things that are not necessary. We manage our finances, account statements, credit balances, invoices, tax returns and invoices. This means you will have too many paper documents in your home. Make sure you organize your documents. If you are an organized person, you probably already have this covered. Even if you're organized, you'll arrive at a point at which paper documents become too much. Decide which documents you want to keep and which documents you want to destroy. Try to keep your tax-related documents for at least seven years, especially if you own a business or are self-employed. Sometimes, the IRS asks for physical documents to prove you have paid your taxes when you check your account. Destroy all irrelevant documents, any unnecessary files, and old and paid bills in your home. Eliminate guarantees, ATM tickets, insurance and investment fund prospects that are no longer valid but that you have lying around. In the financial world, it is estimated that about 80% of the records we hold are never examined. Look for easier ways to get the bills you receive. Apply for electronic invoices, electronic balances and electronic account statements when possible.

Be sure to close accounts you do not need. It could be an open account with former employers or it could be due to your finding a better investment, savings or interest rate. Also sell those things in your garage and your home that you have not used for a long time.

Ready to be successful

This is a vital step. Preparation for success is important for being successful. Observe clear and concise goals. Know what your short- and long-term goals are. Set a certain timeframe for achieving those goals. Talk to your partner or spouse about your goals and financial projections. Getting your spouse on board will ensure that you do not work against any other financial plan. You could also get valuable information about other ways you can achieve your financial dreams. Talk to your accountant if you have one, so you can avoid falling into tax traps and prepare for challenges to achieve your financial freedom.

Obtain your financial data, i.e., reports

Always ask for your financial reports to be sent to you, preferably electronically, to avoid a lot of paper clutter. It is also important to take your time to learn how to read financial statements. Know how to use the information garnered from the reports to gauge your financial health and improve your finances. Your income statements, cash flow and balance sheet tell a story about your financial journey. They enable you to review your expenses and decide whether your assets are bringing in enough money for you. They help you know what your net worth is. When you understand how financial reports work and how to use them in optimizing the ways you spend money, it is incredibly empowering. They can also show any hidden fees and give you an idea of what you are paying. Do not shy away from asking any questions about items on your financial statement that you do not understand.

Evaluation of future income

Determining how much money is available is the key to making financial choices. Prior to creating a budget, it is important that you know the total income. This is because the aim of budgeting is to keep spending below your income. To evaluate how much money will be available to spend, an individual must answer the following:

1. Will your income be from the same source or different sources?

2. How much can you expect to earn in the future?

For people who are working, the largest source of income will be their monthly paychecks. Irregular sources of income are unreliable but should be taken into consideration. Future income will be influenced by customary deductions like income tax and insurance payments. This should be considered to determine the total income that can be counted on.

Evaluation of debts

Since there are many reasons to borrow and many avenues from which to do so, the average individual is likely to be in debt. Freedom from debt is a desirable financial goal to pursue. It begins by evaluating the present debt profile and how it is being managed.

There are many indicators of poor financial management and the need to make debt payments a priority. Some are:

1. Use of an increasing proportion of income for the payment of debts
2. Making only the minimum payments on debts
3. Uncertainty about the actual amount owed
4. Being threatened with or facing actual legal action by creditors
5. Payment of bills with money earmarked for other purposes
6. Late payment of bills
7. Reaching the limit on lines of credit
8. Making more purchases on credit instead of paying with cash.
9. The risk of immediate financial strain if the primary source of income is lost

A good way to approach debts involves making a list of creditors and amounts owed. The annual interest rates and agreed-upon monthly payments should be equally noted in this list. The most important benefit of reducing debt is the absence of emotional, psychological and financial strain on individuals and families, as well as the sense of fulfillment from future financial security. Less debt confers an improved credit profile, which affects applications for jobs, further credit and insurance. It also provides more money for achieving other goals.

Ensure your money counts

Always make sure everything you pay money for is necessary. Avoid spending just for the sake of it. Avoid frivolities as much as you can. Stay away from things that trigger you into buying impulsively. Always negotiate kick-backs and discounts on everything you spend money on. Discounts are a great way of saving a few dollars. Over time, these little reductions on prices create a significant amount of money saved. It is also important to ensure you save these discounts; a good practice is to always transfer the discounted amount immediately into your savings account. For example, if you negotiate a price reduction of two dollars on a smartphone deal, make sure to transfer the two dollars into your savings account. This accomplishes something profound. Many of us tend to be penny-wise and pound foolish; we save a few bucks on a deal, then immediately buy something with that money, something we did not plan, just because we feel a little "richer" at that moment. It also instills in us a saving culture, making us realize that no amount is too little to save.

Take the debt test

Various tests have been designed to help you figure out your level of debt, including how you can keep it under control so that you can focus on getting back on track to making your financial plans work for you. There are a lot of free debt tests on the Internet that you can complete; most of them take less than 10 minutes to complete. They come mostly in the form of structured questions. The results often state what your biggest debts are, how you go about accumulating them, ways you can more quickly pay them off and steps to take to avoid falling back into them. Although not everybody feels comfortable taking these tests, they provide valuable insights and are worth a try.

Debt payment

There are two common approaches to dealing with multiple debts. One is to concentrate on paying off the smallest debt first. This is done while you pay the required monthly payments on all other loans. After that loan is repaid, successive loans with the smallest amounts are paid until the process is completed. This approach is very rewarding, as it allows you to vividly see progress.

Another, more popular, method is to first concentrate on repaying debts that have the highest interest rates. Doing this, you will succeed in avoiding the high interest charges that might have piled up over time. This prevents you from spending more than necessary in servicing your loan before you eventually pay it off. Whatever method you use, however, it is very important that you are committed, persistent and patient in paying off debt.

There is yet another approach toward paying debt, which is to pay off as much as possible in a fast and sudden manner. This depends on your financial capability to pay off the debt and still be able to meet the funding for your expenditures and other financial obligations at the same time. This may require you to work extra jobs. It may also require you to reduce your expenditures by depriving yourself of other activities that cost you money. It should also be known that paying off a debt as soon as possible requires you to pay more than the minimum payments.

In some situations, it is difficult to meet your financial payments. It is then advisable to seek financial advice from an expert, be it a financial consultant or a creditor. Creditors offer solutions in the form of long-term payoff strategies or a debt management plan.

Set priorities

Getting priorities right is an essential part of gaining financial control. Setting priorities increases your resolve to resist the influence of peer pressure and advertising campaigns that promote consumer spending. The trick is to keep your focus on your financial priorities as firmly as possible.

It begins with making a list of items that represent both wants and needs of the individual and family. This list should arrange the items in order of importance. A footnote may be made on why each item is a priority to serve as encouragement to achieve it, as well as to keep priorities in the right perspective. More importantly, relevant needs are addressed before wants, which are unnecessary at the moment. Payments for debts and savings for future short-term and long-term goals should be given the most priority.

A further step is to ensure that you place these lists in places where they can be easily seen, like screen savers, pictures and wallpapers. These serve as personal ads that remind you of your goals.

Know what your needs are. Identify habits that exceed what you truly need or can afford. Know what steps you must take to ensure you have a strong financial base. Strive to live on less than your income. When you know your priorities and stick to them, your financial growth rate will accelerate. You will reduce time wasted in determining your course of action when deciding to spend money on certain things. You will achieve a clarity of purpose and become more financially efficient.

Create sustainable and achievable financial goals

Setting goals and working toward them are critical ingredients for living a successful life. Goals serve as a destination and stop unnecessary distractions. It is important to have goals when undergoing financial planning. More importantly, however, you must set goals that are achievable. They could be challenging, but you need to ensure they are achievable and sustainable. You should also try to set milestones. This will serve to fuel your motivation to stick to the financial plan.

A specific financial goal is a quantifiable result that is desired after a specific timeframe. Examples of specific goals include achieving a net income of $6,000 per month and paying off a mortgage. Measuring financial goals is simple. Most financial goals have a monetary value attached to them. If the goal is specific enough, it will be easy to measure.

While being optimistic is a very good attribute, financial goals should be as realistic as possible. They should be made while keeping in mind the resources at one's disposal and the existing obligations that need to be met. A balance should be struck between pushing oneself to achieve a demanding goal and simply making sound financial choices.

Financial goals should be time-bound. Goals will obviously differ in the length of time required to achieve them. Without a time limit, it is easier to get off track. Goals should be defined as short term, medium term and long term. Short-term goals are those that can be completed in less than two years. Medium-term goals are those that can be completed within two to five years, while long-term goals require more than five years for completion. A short-term goal would be saving for a summer vacation as well as purchasing furniture, while a long-term goal would involve college and retirement savings.

Classify them into short-term, medium-term and long-term goals

After setting achievable goals, structure those goals into short-term, medium-term and long-term goals. The importance of this is so you know what to focus on at every point in time. Thus, you won't end up working on your long-term goals at the expense of your short-term goals. A good practice to undertake is to structure your short, medium and long-term goals so that they are linked and progressively lead one to another. Thus, when working on your short-term goals, you are also laying the groundwork for your mid-term goals. Long-term goals also help sustain your motivation to secure your financial future. You understand that you are moving toward your long-term goals without feeling as though it is a long, tough journey.

Offset your debts

In situations, where applicable, it is wise to consider offsetting debts, especially if they involve a large amount of money. Try to negotiate with the other party on the offset conditions and terms. An agreement could be made in terms of how much to pay and the actual offset value of the debt. This is another brilliant way of reducing your debts.

Plan for the unexpected

It is wise to always set aside emergency funds. While we are always hoping for the best, it is important to plan for unforeseen circumstances. This could be in the form of a job loss, a decline in share returns, health issues and other challenges. Such issues could be severe enough to cause considerable financial strain.

Apart from the known long-term savings, it is advisable that an individual save so he has living costs for the next three to six months. This view is widely supported by experts. It means anticipating the unexpected, which can go a long way toward preventing minor financial issues from escalating into major and complex financial disasters. The action also creates a buffer for things that were hitherto not planned in our budgets. We must also ensure that the things we own are properly insured. This will help foot the bills, be they medical or repair-related, in the event of an accident or any other form of damage to our property. This is safer than dipping into money we could otherwise use for investment, since the insurance policy will cover the medical or repair bills.

Saving

Saving is the lifeblood of your financial success. Endeavour to save constantly. If you find saving difficult, automate your weekly or monthly savings so that when your earnings enter your account, a certain sum is automatically deducted and placed into your savings account. Have a savings account from which you can't easily withdraw money. Also, immediately transfer every discount you get into that savings account so you do not spend it on something else.

Analyze your expenditures

We need to constantly scrutinize where our money goes on a daily, weekly and monthly basis. This allows us to identify patterns in our spending habits and, hence, determine whether they are healthy. Once we have identified our spending patterns, we can create methods of reducing our overall weekly or monthly expenses. We must document our projected desired expenditure over a period of time, be it weekly or monthly. We must be aware of those things on which we might be required to spend money. This also allows us to decide what is appropriate and what is not when dealing with expenses. In addition, we must identify and document our fixed monthly expenditures. These allow us to plan ahead. Such expenses could even be automated so we need not worry about paying them at the end of the month or when they are due.

Perform a financial re-assessment

We should strive to always review our financial plan, to always analyze our journey on the path to financial success. Nothing is set in stone. This activity enables us to realize what works and what doesn't. It helps us create plans and strategies according to the situations with which we are dealing, without losing sight of our goals. We can thus take the necessary steps to actualize those goals.

Understanding the cost of credit

We need to understand the true cost of credit. Most times we are offered credit with terms that give us cash discounts or a percentage off if we pay off the amount within a certain period. It would serve us well to utilize credit like this if we know we can pay it off on time. The eventual costs of loans like this are taken care of by the income from the asset. This allows us to own such assets without upsetting our financial balance.

Chapter 12: Financial Struggles

Suppose you desire a life of blissful freedom in which you feel fulfilled and removed from the fear or stress of whatever it is the world has made of you. What do you think you need? Money? Perhaps. However, what you do need is a sense of security such that you experience no constant worries about people holding a threat over you that may require you to bend to their will. It is this sense of security that drives away nights full of heaving and sighing. You will find that you are healthier and happier and that you rarely need to look over your shoulder out of fear that danger is chasing you. Only one thing can remove all of these things from your life and that is a lack of financial struggle. Financial problems are not just a poor man's thing; there are situations in which a rich man, despite his wealth, may find himself struggling financially.

Money, they say, makes the world go round—metaphorically speaking, of course. The absence of it, though, can lead to worries, stress and sometimes even a nervous breakdown. Why does the absence of money cause us to feel this range of emotion? Why does it shorten our emotional fuse? Is money that important? And even more, how do we avoid a financial crisis?

The very basis upon which materialism stands is money. The desire to own materials does not matter. What matters is your ability to afford the cost of such materials. Typically, people find it almost impossible to satisfy their wants. Because of this, people tend to think that those who do not own material items are poor. They see immaterialism as a direct effect of poverty. This leads to the general belief that minimalism is about becoming poor. These beliefs lead people to think that only those who are poor struggle financially.

The media has been successful in painting an image of financial struggles as being the result of stock fluctuations, inflation rates, the forces of supply and demand, unemployment and other bogus factors. Although these factors contribute to the general statistics when we measure the rate of financial crises or predict future trends in the national financial state, they play a tiny role in our very own financial situations. We see an increase in the prices of goods and services as a causal factor of financial struggle. We never really consider that, upon bitter reflection, we may actually be exhibiting the desire to struggle financially by the way we have structured our consumption. We also fail to notice that most of the materials lying around unused in the attic, basement or garage are serving as waste and liabilities.

Our problem as humans has always been "acceptance." We fail to accept the reality of most things in different ways. When we're told that the way out of our financial challenges is rational materialism, or rather simply minimalism, we allay fears that the economy will crash. What economy? The one we have not lived to witness yet? In this manner, people have found it difficult to accept that they are struggling financially. Rather, they see it as not doing enough, as being not results-oriented or as an inability to function in a manner that society accepts. People rarely sit down to think, 'Why am I in the mess in which I have found myself? What is it that I am not doing correctly?' Rather than finding out how to rectify these issues, we place the blame upon the economy, the government and sometimes ourselves. Blaming is not the right course of action—finding the solution is.

Financial pressure affects everybody at some point in their lives. Nobody is immune from it. The rich and the not-so-wealthy suffer through difficult financial situations. Worrying about how to pay the bills, the status of our investment portfolio and how we can afford to take care of our families all adds up to create intense pressure. Sometimes it could also be a result of bad decisions or mistakes we made previously.

Our financial struggles come from many things and are often a symptom of a much larger problem. Whenever we are feeling financially strained or handicapped, we must take a step back and try to look at the bigger picture so we can understand where in our lives our problem come from.

When we are in financial turmoil, everything seems to go downhill from that point on. The reasons for this are not far-fetched when you are in that state; your emotions take on a negative spin, and you can see only the present situation—not beyond it. This kind of situation causes you to constantly think about even worse scenarios or how badly things could continue to go for you. This type of thought process agitates you, and then you start seeking short-term solutions which provide temporary respite but ultimately worsen your financial position. The remedy most people seek almost immediately is to borrow more money or sell property. While borrowing can increase the cash available in that period, you ultimately end up worse than before because it becomes a burden you also have to pay off.

Apart from a financial crisis's obvious direct consequence, which is a shortage of cash, it can affect your mental and physical health. Constant worries over financial situations inflict stress on the body and have an enormous impact on mental health. People become frustrated at their inability to get out of the situation, which causes a reduced tolerance of co-workers, anger at their colleagues or spouse, violent tendencies, alcoholism, drug abuse and other social vices. This change in the attitude of the individual further alienates him or her from his or her friends and family, who could support, encourage and help.

According to recent studies, people who undergo financial difficulties show a profound change in their appetite and sleeping patterns. During this period, the body reduces its metabolism, releases cortisol, increases the heart rate and blood pressure, suppresses the memory and reduces concentration in its attempt to cope with stress. An increase in cortisol level over an extended period causes weight gain, muscle weakness, a weakened immune system and mood swings. It even even lowers the sex drive, which is a major problem for married couples. This increases the risk of stroke, heart disease, sexual dysfunction and diabetes.

Causes of financial struggle

Having looked into what financial difficulties exist, it is appropriate for us to investigate the causes of financial hardship. Following are a few causes of financial problems, although this list is by no means exhaustive:

Bad financial decisions

This is the most common cause of financial crisis in our lives. People make bad money decisions every day, including lending money they actually need, investing huge sums of money in risky projects or businesses, gambling or even participating in Ponzi schemes. Sometimes a new project is very attractive, so we dive right in and invest our cash and savings into it. It is wiser to step back from that initial euphoria and take a measured, logical approach to the situation.

Sometimes we leave the business of our finances to our attorneys or accountants. These individuals are also human and could make mistakes—and they are very adept at covering them up, especially if their clients have no idea how the financial system works. This is why it is vital to invest time in understanding how to manage your finances. Even if you have attorneys, they will realize that they cannot make stuff up for you because you know how it works and you will ask questions about how they arrived at the figures they presented to you.

Illness or accidents

There is a saying that health is wealth—this is spot on. When we are ill, we are unable to go about our normal day-to-day activities. This could have a massive effect on our income, especially if we run a sole proprietorship business which is our only source of funds. Sometimes people come down with severe diseases like heart conditions or cancer, whose treatments can be expensive. Other times, accidents cause temporary or permanent damage, preventing the patient from carrying out his economic activities. Illness or accident can disrupt even a very well-executed financial plan if the hospital bills are too much to be covered by the insurance policy. This can have further reaching consequences for people without an adequate health care plan or insurance.

Unemployment

Simply put, unemployment is when you do not have a job, task or duty that brings you money regularly. Living comes at a cost. We pay for the food we eat, the electricity we use, our transportation, water, the clothes we wear and the list goes on. How do we pay for these amenities when we do not have a source of income? Unemployment may be due to laziness. Nobody wants to work with a lazy person. They drag on jobs that should have been completed in a lot less time. They are unreliable. Sometimes unemployment is due to the person being unskilled or inadequately skilled for the jobs that are available. Due to competition and the race to survive, companies and businesses would rather employ people who can hit the ground running. Other times, there might be just a simple scarcity of jobs. Mass retrenchments due to machines taking over the bulk of the work humans perform, or a downsizing company, can also lead to unemployment. Whatever the cause, unemployment is a common factor in financial struggles.

<u>Low income</u>

People with jobs occasionally have money problems. This issue is usually brought about when people with low incomes live beyond their means—buying what they cannot truly afford, taking on a bunch of credits cards they cannot pay off on time and even trying to keep up with the Joneses. Sometimes the issues with low income may arise when an individual who was laid off from work accepts another job with less pay just so he or she can stay afloat. Also, when companies downsize they tend to reduce the wages paid to their workers to manage the bottom line and expenses the corporation incurs.

<u>Having a baby</u>

Babies are precious gifts from nature, although they are also expensive to care for. From the time of conception, expecting mothers are supposed to visit the doctor regularly, undergoing checkups so that the baby is in excellent condition at delivery. Complications during and after birth could cause added expenses. Baby food, the preparation of a nursery, diapers and medical care can also strain the economic standing of a family. Once the child starts growing up, tuition fees, clothes and other expenses add to the household budget.

<u>Retirement</u>

Without an adequate retirement plan, necessary expenses might become a financial burden. People with a good retirement plan sometimes end up being asset rich but cash poor; they pay a premium on the assets they have acquired over the years, which could lead them to be cash-strapped and force them to liquidate some of those assets they worked hard to garner.

Divorce

Alimony—money ordered by the court to be paid regularly by a partner to his or her spouse for upkeep—can be costly. A divorce can be a very messy situation, especially when it drags on for a long time. Payments to lawyers for their services during this period could also dent an otherwise strong financial base. Sometimes spouses fight over property; the upkeep of this property could leave the husband or wife in a deep financial mess.

Addiction

When people develop an addiction to something, be it drugs or alcohol, they are always craving the satisfaction they derive from it. A drug addict always wants the feeling of being high, and this damages the normal logical process associated with making good decisions. An addict will always seek to buy more drugs or drink more alcohol regardless of how short of cash they are. Some even end up borrowing just to satisfy this urge.

Attachment

Sometimes we are addicted to things we can no longer afford. It could be a car or a house that we can no longer maintain. Rather than do what is best for our financial health, we stick with that property due to our sentimental attachment to it. Sometimes it might be another person, for whom we can no longer have to pay the bills. Rather than sit down and explain the situation, we pretend everything is fine and sometimes even borrow so the person can keep living an extravagant lifestyle.

Those few cases we have talked about could cause financial crises for people. Sometimes it is a combination of some or all of these causes that leads us to our present financial struggles. We need to always be aware of the decisions we make regarding money. We should be conscious of our income and expenses so we can recognize any potential cause of future financial troubles.

Effects of financial struggle

Financial struggle is highly undesirable if we want to learn the true essence of minimalism. How can you be free from fear if you are struggling financially? After our seemingly brief insight into the causes of a difficult financial situation, it is important that we look at the effects financial crises can have on individuals. Some devastating effects of a financial crisis in the personal life of an individual are listed below.

Stress

Once a difficult financial situation sets in, we find ourselves losing sleep and worrying more about the situation. This causes increased stress in the body. Financial burdens and stress usually come hand in hand. It disturbs us mentally and messes up our hormone levels. How we respond to this situation is very important. More often than not, we seek fixes that add to our stress level. We look for shortcuts and short-term solutions. An increase in stress level has also been shown to increase our possibility of making bad decisions. By making rational choices and being content with owning less, we significantly reduce the tendency to struggle financially. The consequence is that to a large extent, our stress level decreases.

Debt

One sure sign of financial struggle is a huge debt. Most times, this is due to taking loans with very high interest rates and being unable to pay them back as they're due. Our inability to pay them promptly increases the amount of money we end up paying over an extended period. Solving this problem is quite easy; you just need to have an emergency savings fund, stop using your credit card as an extension of your income and have a tracking system for your personal finances. Student credit card debts and loans are examples of debts we could experience difficulty paying off. The credit card should never be an extension of income, and one has to stop viewing it as such. Purchase only things you have the financial ability to buy, and not with your credit card. When you are free of debt, the fear associated with it melts.

Bad credit rating

When we take on extended loans that we are unable to pay back, our credit rating takes a huge blow. This portrays us as very unreliable individuals who do not pay off our loans when they're due. Our bad credit rating deters financial institutions from lending us money when we need it—even though we should not need them to lend us money, as we are minimalists! The only sources from whom we could borrow money in this situation are loan sharks. These loan sharks give loans at very high interest rates, and they always seek security for the loan, as nobody wants to stick out their neck. Loans give birth to more loans, and debt profiling increases.

Reduced lifespan

Financial worries cause stress to the body. The body's response to coping with stress is to increase the blood cortisol level. This increase produces some undesirable changes in the body that could lead to serious health issues. Health issues such as stroke and diabetes are not uncommon among people going through a difficult financial situation. In addition, the constant fear associated with the probable consequences of financial struggle can decrease one's lifespan.

Inability to achieve desires

We all have dreams and hopes. Whenever you find that you are unable to get things you need or visit that place you've always dreamed about, it may be due to your being in a tight financial situation. When we are always drawn back from buying the things we want, it is time to take a very close look at our financial situation.

Low standard of living

A reduced standard of living, which is not a conscious decision, is a sure sign of financial crisis. If you are going for months without the heater on, or if the electricity has been disconnected due to your inability to pay the bills, you are in a serious financial bind. It isn't that a minimalist desires a high standard of living, but the standard of living should not be so low. It is about a lifestyle that frees the mind of constant worry and lofty desires.

Marital issues and divorce

When couples undergo financial crisis, the increased stress due to constant worrying makes each partner very irritable. This, combined with reduced sexual arousal and reduced sexual activities, can cause an enormous strain on a marriage. Sometimes one or both members of the couple may seek emotional relationships outside the confines of marriage. Situations like this have led to the break-up of couples.

Tough parenting

Being a parent is not as easy as we like to think. It becomes extremely difficult when you are unable to care for your kids due to financial strain. They need a balanced diet to be healthy so they can grow. A lack of this could lead to health problems, which incur medical bills. Furthermore, a child could end up compromising his or her moral values just so he or she can afford the things that the parents cannot provide.

It is clear that people do not want to feel a lack of resources in their lives. We want to feel abundance, contentment and happiness. How can we achieve this if we are constantly unsatisfied? How do we find joy in the lives we live? Ultimately, how do we bring joy to the people around us? We bring joy by helping them live fulfilled lives, including catering to their various needs as necessary. This and other questions have plagued humanity from time immemorial—including our desire to influence people, to inspire them, or to be that amazing father or mother to our kids.

How do we achieve things like this if we are constantly battling with financial problems? When all our focus is on getting out of the rot we are in? In a world ruled by money, it is difficult to stay centered. We could always seek new ways of making money. Human beings have even resorted to immoral and callous acts to amass a fortune. Why is this so? Why are some people devoid of the capacity to think about their fellow human beings when they are in the pursuit of material wealth and possessions? The reason is that we are controlled by two powerful base emotions: fear and desire.

Man remains a slave to these two powerful emotions. When these emotions—one or both of them—are strong enough, we have the capacity to rationalize any action we take without any sense of remorse or feeling of accountability. Fear causes us to move or run away from something or a situation, and desire pushes us toward something or a situation. Who could have thought that these apparently base emotions could have such a powerful influence on our attitude and how we see life? A person living in a constant state of fear is always agitated and anxious. Those living in a cloud of constant desires are usually obsessive about things and are easily influenced by occurrences, situations and outcomes.

Financial difficulty always comes with either one or both of these emotions. We may be living in a state of constant agitation at the state of our finances. Even when everything is fine, we worry about tomorrow. We ask ourselves questions like: What if I lose everything I have? What if I end up being broke somewhere along the course of my life? How would I cope if a tragedy befell me? How would I be able to afford that house?

Or we may desire a bigger house, a better car, a more expensive coat. We may desire to be rich. These are things we have all experienced at one time or another. What do we do about those desires? Do we spend all our savings to acquire them? Or do we accumulate so many credit cards that we end up defaulting on their payments? Some would rather go for loans (house loans or car loans) without thinking it through, or without considering how this action will affect their long-term financial goals.

Little seemingly common-sense suggestions can help us out of a bad financial situation. Taking steps like saving a portion of our income or ensuring we pay the minimum monthly amount on all our credit cards will help us stay prepared if anything goes wrong. Another very interesting way to stay prepared is to be a minimalist. If we are minimalists, we will subconsciously take reasonable steps toward gaining freedom from our enslaving desires. Minimalism will provide us with amazing ways to deal with our financial issues and ensure they do not become messy.

Chapter 13: Minimalism is a Solution to Your Financial Struggles

Contrary to widespread popular beliefs about minimalism, it is actually a very profound way of living that eliminates many of the problems that are caused by our desires and fears. Minimalism strives to bring our consciousness toward simple solutions to our everyday struggles. Even though the application of minimalism is quite large in a sense, we will aim to investigate ways in which minimalism improves our financial situation in this chapter.

In the modern world, we have become avid consumers of products. This attitude actually developed before World War II. We were influenced by the media in an attempt to boost the industrial and manufacturing market. We were coerced by the media and advertising agencies into believing that having bigger cars, acquiring expensive houses and wearing expensive clothes were signs of being financially stable. We were conditioned to believe that you command respect, attract the opposite sex and feel confident only if you have these things in your life. The media came up with terms like "retail therapy," so we would associate shopping for new clothes with therapy, i.e. a means of reducing stress. The media compels us to spend more. We feel that if we could only get that new smartphone, we would be happier, or if we could just get those beautiful red shoes, our confidence would soar. Although I have nothing against red shoes or smartphones, you need to ask yourself: "What is the long-term financial cost of buying these items?"

Being a minimalist requires a profound paradigm shift. There is a change in the way we see things and the way in which we approach our desires. Some people think being a minimalist is living a basic life—no smartphones, no computers, no nice clothes. Although there are people who live like this and call themselves minimalists, this perspective is wrong. There are also people with nice cars and beautiful homes who are minimalists. Our basic needs in life—to survive—are actually clothing, shelter and food. That's all. If you have those three covered, you will live. However, due to our evolution as a species, we have refined these living conditions. Rather than staying in a cave, we have built comfortable and lavish homes. We have improved the way we dispose of waste due to its health and environmental impacts. We have also redefined our dietary needs to optimize and ensure we lead healthy lives. Apart from the need for shelter, clothing, food and other basic amenities, everything else is just extras.

Studies have shown that although we need appropriate clothing, we end up wearing only one-third of the clothes we own. What about the remaining two-thirds in the closet? We wear them sparingly. Some people even wear them only once or twice a year. What of shoes, belts, ties? We actually buy more than we need. The media has invented fashion trends, which we are compelled to follow so we can fit into society. What happened to wearing what fits and what we are comfortable in?

It is also difficult to convince friends, colleagues and families that living with less actually leads to financial freedom. The perceived American dream does not seem to follow this line of thought. Now that we live in a society of excess, it has become even easier to try to keep up with the Joneses. Easy access to credit further promotes this mentality. It makes us lose track of our expenses, which ultimately muddles our financial health.

Many people are faced with the seemingly difficult decisions of where and how to start getting a hold of their finances. You may also struggle with this feeling even though the amount of time every individual spends in this state varies greatly. The first step to removing financial troubles with the aid of minimalism is to take responsibility for your situation. You see, your wants and desires exist in your mind and only you have the power to decide whether or not to act on them. Understand that you are in this present financial mess due to the decisions you have made and upon which you have decided to act. Once you have accepted this fact, you need to have a huge paradigm shift. You need to commit to improving your financial situation because without committing and sticking to it, you will regress and carry on with the actions that landed you in this present situation. You need to shift the focus from financial worries to financial freedom. You should speak to yourself and convince yourself about this new perspective, which will become a new approach to living.

After we have completed the step above, we can proceed to one of the most important steps of all, which is to declutter. Decluttering is getting rid of those items that are only extras in our life and do not impact our livelihood significantly. We also need to get rid of those unnecessary things that have a continuous impact on our money, whether monthly or weekly. This step will get rid of those wants you have acquired over the years and leave just the things you need. This process can be quite tough if you are not mentally prepared for it. Like I said before, we humans can rationalize any action when we are under the influence of the emotions of fear and desire. A lot of people ask themselves questions like: What if I get rid of it only to need it later? My answer to this is: If it is not a necessity, you can easily get it later. This makes sense in three ways. One, you will not lose the opportunity cost that you could use elsewhere. Two, you will reduce the risk of keeping something you may not need later. And lastly, you will not feel guilty when you remember that there is something accompanying your budget that you do not need immediately.

When decluttering, the decision regarding what to sell or give away is yours to make, but it is important that you choose those items that are in excess of what you actually need. Decluttering our lives and our homes enables us to spend less time on cleaning. Organizing the house and our household items reduces the amount of money we spend on repairing damaged items we do not use, and it frees up time for us to pursue the activities that inspire us. Moving into a smaller home can also be considered to be a part of decluttering. When a family is starting off, it may need to get a large house to accommodate both the parents and the children. When those children get older, go to college or marry, the parents may find themselves with more space than they need. Moving into a smaller home that serves just the spouses' needs is the smart thing to do. The parents can sell off the larger house to free up cash; the home maintenance fee is reduced and they will pay less on property taxes. The same applies to selling excess items in the house. You would be amazed by the amount you can realize from the sale of those things you do not need.

A study by CNN shows that in America, the average household incurs a debt of $10,700. Most of this is made up of credit card debt, college loans, house loans and car loans. Some studies also show that 63% of the American population cannot deal comfortably with an emergency that costs $500. Another huge amount of this debt goes into buying things that are not a necessity. When you sell items you do not need, the funds you earn can go into repaying your outstanding debts and loans. An excellent way to do this is by listing all the debts you have and arranging them in order from highest to the lowest. Then you want to pay off the small debts on the list. After paying off those debts, prepare a workable automated plan for paying off the bigger debts at the top of your list. Making the process automated reduces the burden of thinking about those debts when you are paying them off. This process is simple. It makes paying off debts easier, but it can be tedious and take a long time if you have huge debts. However, in the end you will have paid them off and become financially stable. When you have achieved this financial freedom, you can then channel this automated process toward ensuring you are always saving a portion of your income.

Minimalism trains your mind to eliminate financial discontent. Reining in your financial fears and outrageous desires makes you calm and centered. You will develop the ability to naturally track how much money is coming into your account, how much you spend on things and what those things are. It will enable you to put yourself in check when you discover you are drifting from your grand financial plan. Cultivating this habit, over time, builds your confidence and puts your mind at ease. What else is minimalism if not a new set of habits? In the course of your journey through life while living as a minimalist, you will discover that it is possible to live with less money and still be happy. The feeling of not having enough money has its roots in the desire for luxuries we cannot afford or that don't match our income. We then conclude that if we only make more money, we will be happy. However, we discover that when we make even more money, we start yearning for other things beyond our increased income. It is a circle that never stops unless we develop a disciplined mind, live frugally and avoid things that are not a necessity.

The feeling of being in charge of our financial destiny makes us happy. This is a very powerful and enabling feeling to have. It re-energizes us and fuels our passion for pursuing meaningful activities in our lives. It is a known fact that when you are happy, you develop a tendency to be positive. You see possibilities in every new experience in your life. You are also driven to contribute to the happiness of others, to inspire them to become high achievers and to help those who may be going through difficult financial times.

When you can pay off your debts, you can take control of your financial life and build confidence. This will increase your overall credit rating. With this improved financial situation, you will have the freedom to use loans creatively. For example, you might see a nice property that you could use to generate passive income while you are still working. Sourcing loans to finance a venture like this allows you to key into opportunities when the need arises. This is also an example of a good debt in the sense that it ultimately pays off the debt incurred from the income it generates. Having built a system for the repayment of debts over time, this places little to no financial strain on one's budget.

Minimalism also allows us to avoid frivolities we can do without. Sometimes in our jobs or business, we feel like we are trapped. We feel incomplete. Most times this feeling stems from the need to keep up appearances. When we strive to live such a lifestyle, we often end up in debt and lose the respect and the credibility that has been accorded to us. We take on large mortgages, take one huge car loans and buy expensive clothes we can do without. Minimalism teaches us to discipline our minds toward impulses like this. It reinforces our self-sufficiency and independence.

It also makes us seemingly immune to the influences of the media. Whenever new products are thrust in our faces or pressed upon us, we ask ourselves if we need this item, if the desire to get this item is just to keep up appearances. Whenever our colleagues or friends push us to do things that could hamper our financial well-being, we can laugh and politely tell them no. This is because we have built enough mental strength to be confident in our skin, to make decisions that serve us and make our lives better. People associate buying less as a backward step in their lives. You as a minimalist understand that this is a limiting belief and that buying less actually leads to abundance. We have more energy, less clutter in our houses, less clutter in our minds and an increased amount of wealth.

Struggles with minimalism

Leading a less stressful life with the aid of minimalism increases our happiness. Medical practitioners agree that a happy individual experiences an increase in his or her physical and mental health, is much less prone to diseases, possesses a stronger immune system and lives a longer life. Being a minimalist is a journey during which you must continuously review and examine your life, review the things you value and constantly adjust to changes. However, the path to becoming a minimalist is not a smooth one. Some of the issues people struggle with when striving to be a minimalist are stated below.

Starting out

The biggest hurdle you will face on the path of minimalism is in the beginning. Getting started can be quite a grueling affair. How do you explain to your friends and colleagues about the new life philosophy you have adopted? How do you rationalize the decision to buy less when buying more is the norm? How do you explain to your wife that getting that new coat is an expense she can do without? How do you make your husband see that the car he is planning to buy is not necessary or explain to your son that the high-tech gaming PC is not needed? These issues and others will come up when you begin this journey.

Human beings are initially resistant to change. Eventually, they accommodate change and even promote it later on. This has occurred in all advancements we have experienced as a species. You need to ask yourself why you want this. Focus on what changes you need to make in your life. You need to see being a minimalist as saying YES to things that add value to your life instead of saying NO to things. This shifts your perspective from the negative to the positive. Concentrate on this aspect of saying yes to experiences rather than saying no to things. Keeping this fact in mind helps you work through resistance or even mockery from other people. It is these same people who will later celebrate you and ask how you did it when you achieve the financial freedom and happiness you deserve. Be polite but firm in this decision you have taken because it is crucial to your success.

Maintaining a sustainable approach to consumerism

Once you decide to declutter and to remove all excess material things in your life, some things will begin to crop up and make you want to compromise. The pull to spend on things we do not need soars within us. How do we deal with this pressure when it becomes unbearable? This is why we need to unclutter our minds first when we journey on this path of minimalism. Our minds will play terrible tricks on us if we do not discipline them. We must first de-clutter our minds by releasing them from the grip of the desires and fears in our lives. This enables us to declutter our lives without stress. We will be able to rid our minds of limiting thoughts, like the belief that more money would make us happier, or more clothes would relieve us of the stress we feel in our daily lives. These are tricks that the mind plays on us to draw us back into our destructive ways. Consumerism was promoted to avert the problem of overproduction in the 20th century and it is still a problem in our present society.

It is funny that while buying stuff makes us happy, at least for a period, owning stuff does not. We need to be true to our resolution to not buy things we don't need and to be steadfast in the face of an overwhelming urge to go on a spending spree. We should realize that all of these things exist only in the mind. Minimalism is about consciously living a fulfilled life rather than a restricting one. Try not to be too frugal, or to start off by living a completely spartan life. You want to spend part of the money you have saved on activities you enjoy. This will make you realize that you can have fun, feel satisfied and derive pleasure without possessing or buying things you don't need. It will reinforce experiences over possessions.

Feelings of guilt when getting rid of expensive items

When we start to declutter our lives and try to rid ourselves of those excesses, we sometimes feel that some items were obtained at a high price. This kind of thinking makes us feel guilty about letting them go. We may start to think about the troubles we went through when getting these items or the hurdles we had to overcome so that we could acquire them. We then feel reluctant about giving them away. We need to understand that these feelings are normal and should be acknowledged. However, it would be a great folly to give in to them. We should realize that we are experiencing these things because of the conditioning that our minds have gone through over time. Resist the impulse to be judgmental or self-critical about those thoughts. Just acknowledge their presence. Know that minimalism is so much more than getting rid of things; it is about creating space in your life and your home for newer experiences rather than things. This simple act lessens the pull of these emotions, and we gradually become free of them. It is also helpful to remind ourselves that we are doing this for ourselves and our future, so that we can live a contented and happy life.

Loss of memories associated with some items

As humans, we are emotional beings. We attach meaning to things. When we undergo this exercise in impressing our feelings on things, we are actually giving them the ability to alter our moods. When we become sentimental toward things, we develop a great attachment to them. When we start living as minimalists and seek to remove from our lives those things that have become excess to what we really need, sentiment becomes a huge roadblock. We can develop attachments to almost anything. Maybe it is that baseball bat your grandfather bought for you on your tenth birthday or the broken surfboard you took to the beach on the day you met the love of your life. The point is, it could be anything at all. What we need to realize is that when we have memories we cherish, we can always relive them. The human mind is a powerful tool. When we visualize our memories in great detail, we begin to feel those things we felt when that incident occurred in the distant past. Getting rid of an item that has become part of clutter in your life does not erase these memories. The irony in this is that when we remember those events, our focus becomes so intense that we begin to see everything that happened that day, which is much more engaging.

Feeling that some items cannot be replaced

Sometimes our minds ask us if we can ever afford (in the future) the items we are getting rid of. This happens especially when we are having trouble paying our bills while living a lifestyle of minimalism. Other times it may be that this particular item is a rare one or a collector's item. You need to realize that the decisions regarding how and what to give away or even when to declutter are ultimately yours to make. Your decision is the only thing that matters. Do not feel pressured into doing it, just ease into it.

Teaching children about having less

Our attitudes, behaviors and lifestyles influence what our kids become as they grow up. We as human beings, especially as children, pick up things subconsciously from other people when we spend enough time with them. This is a good way to influence children when they are still young. You should make it obvious to them through your attitude that minimalism is the best philosophy to live by.

On the other hand, dealing with teenagers can be a very dicey issue. To be quite honest, it is difficult; especially if you are financially well off. They will ask questions that challenge the decisions you make on a logical level. They will ask questions like: Why do you choose to not get me these things even though I know you can afford them?

When we are struggling financially, it is easier to explain things to them simply by saying, "We cannot afford it right now." However, when we are wealthy, this explanation fails. It is important that we have a set of values we stick to and can explain to others when the need arises. When teenagers understand that joy, self-confidence and esteem cannot come from material things, they will develop a profound paradigm shift. This change in their perception of things will make it easier for you to connect with them so that you can work together toward living a fulfilled and happier life.

Scarcity approach to items

Another major struggle people go through in their journey toward becoming minimalists is the scarcity mindset. They think once they sell or give away an item, they will encounter a situation that requires its use. This is what I like to call the "just in case" syndrome. We feel that someday soon we just may need this particular item. The truth is, situations like this rarely happen. Even if they do happen, there are always ways of resolving issues. For example, we could borrow the thing from our neighbors or friends, or we could find creative ways to utilize the items we decided to keep in the process of decluttering our houses. An important shift in your mindset occurs when you look into your reasoning for keeping the things you have. You will discover that you are keeping some things that you rarely use for silly reasons.

Most people stumble upon minimalism only when they have a financial crisis in their lives. They adopt this approach to living and then never look back or have cause to regret the decision they have made. If you are that person, you are going to feel the motivation intensely until you dive headlong into being a minimalist. However, it is important to note that change does not occur overnight and sometimes the process can be slow. You need time to change your mindset and unlearn those habits that have placed you in your current precarious situation.

Some people deal with this decision by thinking they simply need to be more efficient in organizing everything they have. They develop a foolproof system of organization that keeps everything in place—or so they think. Organization may not be a solution to your problem. Those things you keep in place or stack in a room will creep back into your life. When you have decided to declutter your life, do not rush this phase. Consider everything you own carefully. List everything you own, then create a table with the headings KEEP, GIVE, SELL and TRASH. This will give you valuable insight into the things you need in your life. Then act according to what you have written down. Give away what you do not need and what you feel would benefit others. Sell those things you feel are worth selling. This frees up more cash for you. Then incinerate or trash those things you listed under TRASH without any feelings of remorse. They will not contribute to your happiness, so dispose of them. Another very good action to take before decluttering is packing away everything for a week and living with just the essentials. This act will train your mind to creatively use the things you have. You will find new uses for items you haven't previously thought about, and decluttering will become easy for you. Also, constantly review those things you have chosen to keep and decide which items you rarely use. Do the same thing with them. When you are constantly decluttering and letting go of excess items, the process will become a second nature in which you will not have to think too much before disposing of something.

Another way to really get into minimalism after decluttering is to feel more gratitude for the things you own—to feel a sense of joy and happiness in knowing that everything you now have is something you value and love. You really want to enjoy the time you spend with family and friends. Value the time you dedicate to those activities that you are passionate about. Sometimes, without decluttering, those excess items in our lives create a false value system; we feel passionate about things we do not really value. This change in perspective allows us to value life more and to dedicate it to meaningful experiences.

We might struggle with minimalism if we keep comparing ourselves to others based on what they own or what we own. This is the major cause of discontentment. Discontentment breeds unhappiness, jealousy, envy and other bad emotions that destroy us. You will keep chasing things if you constantly compare yourself to others on a purely material basis. Learn to appreciate what you have. Understand that having less doesn't make you less of a man or woman. Understand that your endless pursuit of desires is just a quest to make yourself happier, and that you can achieve this without having lots of material possessions. Happiness exists within. It is intangible. Material things never fully provide happiness. They may, in fact, increase your unhappiness. Everyone is different. Everyone is unique. What goes well for others may not go well for you. Own yourself, embrace your individuality; your happiness is what matters most.

When starting on your journey, decide specifically what your goals are, what you want this journey to bring forth in you. Doing this makes tracking your progress easier. It changes the experience from one long, boring journey into milestones and achievements. If we do not state our goals specifically, we will not know whether we have achieved them. If you define your goals in ambiguous statements, you will lose track of your progress. For example, if you have a goal like losing weight, this is ambiguous. What happens if you lose just 10 pounds in a month? Or 20 pounds in three months? However, if you state that you want to lose 20 pounds in a month, you would be able to track your progress accordingly. This step allows you to revel in your achievements. It also gives you the power to reflect on your journey, decide exactly where you want to end up and plan the appropriate course of action.

If you are a chronic shopper or buy a lot of things impulsively, I would advise you to stay away from malls, shopping centers and online stores as much as you can. If you constantly remain in touch with things that trigger this attitude, you can easily get sucked into your old habits. Our society attributes going to the mall or shopping centers as a means of socialization. Our friends call us up on the weekend for a shopping spree. Sometimes we find ourselves in stores, checking out items and thinking about how amazing it would be to buy them. When you start feeling like that, beware; you are getting sucked back into the buying mentality. Stay away from online stores, too. If need be, install apps that block you from accessing those websites. It would be much better to spend time with your friends in a park or do something similar. Unlike shopping, activities like this increase and solidify your bonds with friends and family.

It is also helpful to focus on owning less rather than throwing out things. This allows you to be more critical of the things you bring into your home. You will scrutinize those things thoroughly and only bring items you value and appreciate into your life. Doing this, you will realize that you require fewer things to make yourself truly happy. You will also develop an appreciation for the little things of life, for the relationships you keep and the experiences you have.

People with children rationalize keeping some stuff by telling themselves that they are saving it for their children. Experience has shown that children often do not want their parents' stuff. Some see it as being "old school," which is not "cool." Sometimes the world has moved past these items to better ones that are more efficient and perform a wider range of functions. Therefore, stop using excuses like that. Be brutally honest with yourself when decluttering.

It is not uncommon to see a minimalist cutting down on waste. Minimalism reduces the waste we produce because we cut down on our excesses. Over time, minimalists have become more environmentally conscious. Some people I know who are minimalists have started gardens, where they grow food and lead a less stressful life. Over the course of their journey as minimalists, many people leave their demanding jobs to seek jobs that are less stressful. This frees up time for them to pursue activities they enjoy. They feel less pushed to pursue a career. Rather, they engage in jobs they enjoy. They are able to work, earn money and be happy doing it. A recent study suggested that people who engage in jobs they love constitute less than 35% of a country's population. Most people are stuck in jobs they would rather not perform. They grumble when the day breaks because they must resume the work for which they have no passion. When you work on something you loathe, you do not put your heart and mind into it. Your productivity drops and you end up producing poor work. How awesome would it be to work at a job you love, to not worry about money and to have enough time to pursue your other interests? That is the joy most people feel when they become minimalists.

Chapter 14: A Minimalist Economy

In the face of the ever-increasing numbers of minimalists, a new fear has taken over most of the world's economists, as many have attempted to predict what will be the eventual outcome of the economy should the population of minimalists become a majority. Their conclusions, although with a little difference here and there, were unanimous; the world economy will crash if people develop the desire to own less. In truth, the questions raised about the effects of the surge of a minimalist economy are important ones. What if everybody chose to become a minimalist? What would happen to our economy? What are the implications?

The arguments of the people are simple. Our national and collective well-being requires the populace at large to buy things we really do not need. If the minimalist economy should take over, our economy will be ruined (according to them). In ordinary terms, this means we all have to be perpetual consumers for the economy to survive. The key word here is "overconsumption." To the world, our desire to own more and chase after material wealth is the solid foundation on which the economy of the country rests. By saying that people should stop being irrational consumers, we are asking that the basis of the economy be removed. The outcome of this development is that our economy would come tumbling down to our feet while we watch. The problems with this argument are numerous, but the most outstanding one is the assumption that minimalism is solely about the desire to own less. We know this is a typical half-knowledge perspective. Minimalism is more than just the desire to own less.

A typical statement that can be seen in the economic journals these days is "People have to keep spending. If the people are to gear more effort toward their savings and tailor down on their debt, the economy will crumble and there is nothing anyone will be able to do about that." Another key word we should focus on here is "debt." Apart from being perpetual and irrational over-consumers, the economy needs us to be in constant debt for it to survive. As questionable as these arguments may sound to us, they are the bitter reality of how our economy has been functioning for a long time. Our argument here is not to question the rationality of these occurrences or criticize them. Our objective in this part is to study humans' conception of the economy in the advent of minimalism.

We have established something in the last paragraph; the economy thrives on both "overconsumption" and "debt." The general public believes that minimalism is out to put an end to these two things, which will supposedly derail a thriving economy. Despite these assumptions, the idea of minimalism has continued to thrive as more people have shown an interest in this perspective and philosophy. Could it be that people have less fear about a crumbling economy? Or could it be that people know these assumptions are not entirely true? What kind of economy needs debt for sustenance? How long can this type of economy last?

The first point of the argument is the flexibility of the economy. To a large extent, it is a common assumption that markets and business dictate the economy. This is true to a certain degree. Marketers, through their system of long hours of work, make good money by shaping the way consumers behave. The marketer fashions production (whether goods or services) to get consumers to reason in a way such that they continue to buy more of the marketer's goods and services. However, business is mostly about meeting the demand of the consumer and answering the core economic questions of what is necessary to produce, for whom to produce it, where to produce it and how to produce it. It should be noted that attempting to answer these questions leads toward one basic fact—that business should be shaped to meet the needs of the consumer. Business should align in a way such that it meets the consumer's behavior and not the other way around (which is what marketers prefer).

Now let us try to create a scenario with interaction between these two things while considering how they affect market prices and the economy at large. To have the consumer buy more of a particular product, the marketer tries to make the consumer behave in a particular manner by having the business produce cheap products at low prices, which is common. To do this, a host of workers somewhere are being underpaid to ensure that the production cost of such a good or service is minimized to meet the demand of the low selling price. These underpaid workers spend less, and the collective effect of their presence does not in any way cripple the economy over a long period. The result is that there are more low-quality products on the rise in the market and the utility derived from these products is greatly reduced. They get damaged or spoilt within a short time and then require replacement. In general, it is not about owning more because you have lots of things lying around. It is about owning more because the ones you already have are damaged or spoilt. The marketers, in this way, dictate consumer behavior by getting them to buy more.

What if, however, consumers decided that enough is enough and they are no longer interested in buying cheap products? They would show a desire to pay more and get maximum utility for their money. In the event of this occurrence, the workforce would be adequately paid. This means the consumers are a factor in deciding the path of businesses and the marketers are not dictating the behavior of the consumers. With the theory of supply and demand, however, this is hardly possible. It is a known theory that consumers will demand more at a lower price and that producers will tend to produce more to meet this increased demand. It's unlikely that consumers will pay more, for a normal good or service, if the price can actually stay low. This is the behavior the marketers have come to recognize, and it is on this basis that they can get the consumer to behave in desirable ways through exploitation. In technical terms, the business economy continues to survive.

In the face of a minimalist community, there is rationality at play. A minimalist will pay the right price for utility. It does not matter what the marketer is offering; a minimalist is not ready to pay unnecessarily to get what he or she does not require to be happy and healthy. There is no way the marketers can get this consumer to behave the way they want. What we have is a community of people who are ready to spend more to get maximum value. It becomes extremely difficult to pull the behavior of these people away from the minimalist perspective. They want to be free of financial insecurity and of debt, so they have decided to pay their dues once and enjoy for a very long time. Price is no longer a determining factor, as it has been replaced by quality. The obvious truth is that when quality is the deciding factor, quantity suffers. This is perhaps why there is a general paranoia that minimalism is all about owning less. We must not forget that economists are of the opinion that consumers need to spend irrationally to keep the economy going.

When all you need is freedom and happiness, as in the case of minimalism, the tendency to be in debt reduces and may even be removed. When your desire to purchase vainly is under check, it is only logical that you will be financially secure. Why do you need to be in debt then? It is good to note here that most minimalists do not see the credit card as an extension of their income and, as such, they do not purchase fervently with it. This is debt reduced to the barest minimum. In a world in which (according to its economists) public debt is needed to foster the economy, this is a challenge. Knowing all of this, one can understand the fear that the economy will be ruined in the face of minimalism. However, all of these assumptions are wrong.

Minimalism and the economy

Now that we have closely examined the possible events caused by the existence of a minimalist economy, we can critically look into the effects of minimalism in a normal economy. Aside from the unnecessary fear that the economy will crash in the face of minimalism, let us have a reflective mind and flexibly examine the possible events that could apparently be conceived in the economy. It is important to note that it is not that the minimalist doesn't spend at all; it is rather a more disciplined approach to rational spending and not spending beyond one's capabilities. It is spending in such a way that you do not negatively affect your financial, mental and emotional capabilities. So, what do minimalists tend to spend on?

With the emergence of a minimalist economy and its continual expansion (and it will keep expanding), the economist should stop promoting the fear that money will no longer be spent. Money will still be spent. What we are looking to see is a shift of focus from some sectors of the economy to other sectors. The consumer, in their usual manner of dictating the "what to produce" answers, will get the manufacturers (now more like entrepreneurs) to shift their attention to the sectors in which they are willing to spend money. To fully understand this, let us take a look at the incidents that occurred with the advent of corporate law.

In the mid-1900's, companies didn't take over other companies, and there were hardly any lawsuits against corporate entities. Companies did not have to pay large sums of money to lawyers billing them by the hour for merely shuffling paperwork, as we see them do now. The lawyers who practiced corporate law then were poor. A few years later, after the great financial crisis, the world economy took on a different form and something unpopular in the business world began spreading among every person who spoke about business in the States. Companies began to take over companies and became conglomerates that were big enough to survive another financial crisis. Corporate law came into the limelight and the old lawyers who had been practicing it for all their careers suddenly became experts and were in constant demand. The most successful lawyers of the late 1900's did not necessarily go to the best schools. They were merely ready for economic change.

In a similar way, this kind of paradigm shift of the economy will occur when the minimalist population reaches a tipping point. The minimalists will spend, but on more important and rational things. Understanding this, we can now discuss the things that will receive more consumption in the event of widespread minimalism.

Food and agriculture

Food consumption will either remain unchanged or receive a boost. No matter what lifestyle people choose to live, they will always eat. What may happen here, however, is that some food will be favored over others. Minimalism is about freedom, not just from fear but from all financial, emotional, mental and environmental issues. Minimalists will have time for themselves, which means they will have freedom to pursue an adventurous life. People in the face of minimalism may decide to eat more organic food than non-organic food. If you have the time to cook yourself a nice dinner, why would you eat processed food from a chemically preserved can or plastic? Why would anyone who is careful about his or her health use things that increase the chances of getting cancer?

Once people decide to consume more organic food, the direct result will be that agriculture will receive an appreciable boost because more farm products will be consumed. However, the boost in the agricultural sector will bring about a rational reduction in the production rate of the agro-allied manufacturing sector and especially the food processing industry. This effect will be seen in two major forms. The first is that there will be a massive reduction in the availability of the agricultural raw materials required by these food processing companies because people (in this case, minimalists) will prefer to consume this farm produce directly (without it undergoing chemical processing). The second effect will be seen in a reduction in the consumption of processed foods. People who are now consuming fresh organic foods will reduce their consumption of processed food. However, it should be noted that neither of these two factors can be completely perfect. There will be only a reduction and not a total abolishment.

Let us examine this as a set of basic economic questions. We begin with "what to produce?" The minimalist masses will have already answered this question: "Produce more healthy/organic food and less processed food." The shift that might be experienced here is that the focus will be on agriculture and other methods of storage rather than food processing. The economists and manufacturers will have to survey the opinions of the masses to determine how many people are absolute minimalists, minimalist vegetarians or just material minimalists. This way, they will be able to figure out how much they need to produce.

Experience

The great thing about minimalism is that it ensures good living. In the wake of minimalism taking over, people will spend more on expressive events that give them bliss and peace of mind. Attending concerts and eating out once in a while will take over. Sporting events will also receive more attention. This is the direction toward which spending will head. The economic shift will favor the entertainment industry, as more concert tickets, sports tickets and theatre tickets will be sold. More people will derive satisfaction from experiences rather than material things. People will seek the kind of bliss associated with attending these events with friends and family. Minimalists, as already discussed, are about being free to do all of these things and spending more time with family and friends.

Travel and tourism

According to anecdotal evidence, many minimalists speak of traveling as an ultimate experience, the very epitome of a pleasurable lifestyle, while many others embrace the lifestyle simply for the pursuit of it. There are others who see it merely as a consequence of owning less. Minimalists appreciate life and have a deep sense of gratitude for everything. Regardless of perspective, the impacts on the travel and tourism economy will be positive and significant. The aviation and transportation industries will receive a boost due to an increase in the number of consumers who purchase their services. Tourism will also be bolstered as people fully maximize their holidays and vacations. Theme parks, recreational centers, wildlife protection sites and game reserves are a few of the venues that will become more prominent. In addition, the industries required to support this industry will be positively affected. The manufacturers of vehicles, oil companies, sport promotion companies and so on are some of these supporting industries.

Art

Many authors speak of art alongside tourism, but in this e-book, we have decided to treat it separately because not every minimalist sees himself as an artist either actively or passively. That is, some can take an active part in art by practicing it while others take part passively by showing appreciation for works of art. Although not all minimalists fall into either of these two categories, there is still little doubt that a higher value will be placed upon art in the face of a new minimalist economy. Because of the freedom of time and mind, people can practice more art because the bliss they feel allows them to channel the figments of their imagination and express them in their fingers. Those who can't practice will tend to show more appreciation for art.

Services

In the face of a minimalist economy, services will receive more attention than retail products. I spoke to a minimalist friend who recently hired a chef, a yoga teacher and a gardener. He credited his ability to hire to minimalism, as he has the financial means to afford these services. Although this is an anecdote, it is widely believed that more of this will happen when most people become minimalists. People will spend less money and time on material things. Thus, they will have the space in their schedules and the means in their budgets to afford these services. They will consider these services as investments in their health, well-being and productivity in the long run.

Individual entrepreneurship will increase as people with special skills find themselves sufficiently employed. Even if they (the service providers) are minimalists themselves, it will still be a win-win situation, as these types of job are stress-free and allow people to do more of what ultimately interests them.

Savings and investment

In addition to savings and investments, business research and problem-solving will be positively affected. Savers and investors are the rocket fuel of the economy, and an economy of minimalism will see an influx of savers and investors. This, in turn, will facilitate more business research and problem-solving. To put it technically, the sacrificing of current consumption will allow people to put more money into the banking sector, either as savings or shares. These investments will end up in the hands of entrepreneurs with new or existing businesses. The entrepreneurs can then use the money to create new, advanced and sophisticated technology, build factories and hire more human capital. All of this will allow them to increase the productivity of goods and services that minimalism requires. Capital is the creator of productivity and productivity controls the standard of living.

Survival-oriented consumer products

The very basis of living itself requires us to consume. We need some basic materials to succeed regardless of whether we are minimalists or generalists. We need shelter, food and clothing. These are the three basic elements of survival and good health according to social science. Minimalists also care about fulfilling their passion, living a life of purpose and staying healthy. All of this requires material goods, which is why we explained that minimalism is not total or complete immaterialism. It is not that minimalism prevents us from purchasing any material goods at all; rather, it requires that we consume higher quality goods that provide maximum utility. In a minimalist economy, human desirability will tend toward premium goods rather than luxurious or exotic goods.

Technology

Like we discussed earlier, minimalism is synonymous with stress-free living, and nothing ensures freedom from stress as much as technology. Minimalism will affect the technology industry in the same way civilization did. People, in their bid to make life easier, will favor the consumption of quality technological products that return value for their money. The integration of all systems into the internet and computer world has already created a path for this. In a minimalist economy, people will share more (banking and philanthropy), reach out more to others (communication), experience the bliss of recreation (entertainment industry to include gaming and sports) and share experiences. This will bolster the consumption of premium and consumer technological products. However, luxurious tech-based products will receive less attention as the desire to own such products is included in the ideals of materialism.

Benefits of a minimalist economy

Apart from the sectors that consumption will increase through the existence of a majority minimalist economy, there are other economic benefits that minimalism will create.

Quality over quantity

The first benefit is that quality will be valued over quantity. The term "minimalism" does not denote that people will have less money to spend; people will still earn money, as they would do in any economy. Money circulation within the economy will remain the same. However, because of the tendency and desire to own less, owning something of quality and flexibility will be valued. The sector that will benefit most from this point of view is the technology industry. Instead of purchasing cheap technological devices (e.g., computers, cell phones and their accessories) that break within weeks of purchase, people will buy devices that last for a long time, even if those devices cost more. In the long run, the cost of purchasing four devices within a year (i.e., four $25 devices that add up to a cost of $100, not factoring in the possible increase or decrease that prices may have suffered as subsequent purchases were made due to economic fluctuations and competition) will be higher than buying one device per year (i.e., for $50). Also, because there would be a shift toward products of higher quality, manufacturers would maximize the use of available resources.

Reduction in waste

Waste has been an issue in our society for a long time. Experts have tried to figure out the best ways to manage waste, to properly dispose it and to even avoid it. The issue of waste management exploded in the industrial age, when consumerism developed. If we were sincere with ourselves, without mincing words, we would realize that some of the things we buy break within weeks or simply fall out of style. Some of these materials are intended to break so that we will buy more of them. (If you disagree, you should read more on planned obsolescence.) The spike in our desires caused a corresponding increase in the volume of materials that were produced by the industries, which in turn caused an increase in industrial waste. On the other hand, consumers discovered that the satisfaction derived from these items was fleeting and it was better to chase newer and "better" products. This led to more consumer waste. In our modern society, and with the evolution of technology, there is an increase in technological waste. We have not been able to deal with the wastes generated during the industrial era properly and now we are piling our current technological waste on top of that. Humans have always sought ways to maximize the use of resources. In a minimalist economy, because people would tend to use fewer material things and be more service-oriented, there would be a drastic reduction in the amount of industrial and technological waste. People would seek out enriching experiences rather than physical products.

Minimalism helps to prevent waste because people avoid companies that flood the market with cheap materials intended to break down within a short period of time. Rather, consumption will favor companies that build things to last. The minimalist buys fewer things and as a result disposes of fewer things. Thus, there will be a proportional reduction in the amount of environmental waste polluting the economy.

Emergence of new technology

With a shift in economic focus, there will be creation of new technologies that will improve productivity and service delivery in the sectors where the focus is concentrated. It should be noted from our earlier discussions that these sectors have hitherto not received general attention, which makes the curve of technological development shift a bit away from them. In an effort to improve the output rate or service quality in this sector, more research will be carried out to create better and improved technology that aligns with these sectors. More funds will be diverted toward researching and developing technological tools, methods and services that ultimately give us a richer experience as human beings. This shift toward research and development will also increase our human capital investments.

Growth of local businesses and services

Because of financial security and freedom of time, minimalists can take advantage of services that a generalist may not be so interested in. The people who offer these services can be individuals or local businesses, and they will experience a significant growth in demand. Also, most of the things you have lying around your house are made in distant countries where it is quite easy to produce cheap products with an even cheaper cost of production. The concern about quality will make people aware of the places where their products come from. This will lead people to purchase local materials that are of good quality and that were produced in great working conditions. The appreciation for local businesses is in itself a plus for the economy, as more revenue can be generated internally from these businesses. Often, local businesses find it difficult to compete with overseas products due to their prices, which differ as a result of their disparate costs of production.

More self-control and reduced crime

Self-control is arguably one of the basic problems people experience in society. Issues concerning health (especially addiction), money (especially debt management and decision-making) and relationships have been found to be deeply rooted in a lack of self-control. The mind or the body desires something, and without giving it as much as an iota of rationality, we go ahead and get it. Two things might happen. The first is that we provided these things for the mind or body and ended up getting ourselves neck deep into problems we could have avoided had we controlled our desires and emotions. The second is that we enter a frenzy of searching for the means to provide these things, knowing full well that we are not currently capable of meeting such wants. However, minimalism gives us the ability to improve our self-control. When we purge our souls of unnecessary desires, we will gain more control over our lives. By learning to think before purchasing things, coupled with our ability to decide to live with less when everything in our nature as humans demands that we live with more, we begin to exhibit a great deal of self-control, which might grow to affect other aspects of our lives. It is easy to live life like that of the king on a chessboard. But one false move can checkmate the king. Therefore, it is better to think before you move.

People without a rational degree of self-control can lose it easily. Most criminals (social vices, not organized crime) do not think about their actions before they act. According to a report by criminologists Richard Wright and Scott Decker, who interviewed 86 convicted armed robbers, the responses given by the criminals were like the following:

"I would try not to think of getting caught. It's too much of a distraction. You can't concentrate on anything if you keep thinking about what is going to happen if it doesn't go right. When I had made up my mind to do a robbery, I would be focused on that and nothing else."

These people do not think about consequences. They do not have any control over their minds or bodies to stop them from committing an evil act. They are driven by their impulses. Because they have damned the consequences, the act (and not their reasoning) controls them. In an economy that encourages self-control, it is possible that we will see a reduction in the crime rate. In addition, minimalism encourages contentment, and in the face of rational desires, it can help shape the orientation of petty criminals. Why steal something you don't need? Why rob a store when there is nothing you desire that requires you to have too much money?

In conclusion, minimalism will ultimately give you a peace of mind that cannot be matched by any material thing.

Chapter 15: Financial Management for Businesses

Financial management can be explained as the process by which we manage our financial resources, which includes management decisions that concern accounting, financial reporting, forecasting and budgeting. It can be defined as the effective and good use of financial sources. It allows the generation of profits, business preparations, acquirement of funds, profit management and sources of revenue. According to the free encyclopedia, it is the efficient and effective management of money to achieve the objectives of an organization, individual or entity. Financial management comprises long-term planning, i.e., for the future to ensure the positive cash flow of an individual, business or entity. The processes involved in financial management include administration and maintenance of financial assets and liabilities as well as the identification and management of risk. Financial management is a vast subject and cannot be captured by just one definition. Many have tried to capture the meaning of financial management in their own words. Some of them are given below.

Another popular definition of financial management is to define it as the activity of management that is concerned with the planning, procurement and control of a firm's financial resources. Financial management relates to the area of a business or the administrative functions of a business that deal with the strategic arrangement of cash and credit. This way, a business can have the means and resources to achieve its set objectives and goals. It offers business owners and managers a lens to determine the progress, viability, stability and consistency of the business while there are various business activities going on, such as sales, procurement, loans and capital investments.

From an investment point of view, Ibrar Alam's definition caught my eye. He defined financial management as the "proper and efficient use of money." He also said it plays a major role in the analysis involved in investing in a profitable business enterprise. Thus, the return on investment must be far greater than the invested amount. Vinod, on the other hand, injected a fresh point of view, as he stated that financial management is functional not only in business but can also be used for every expenditure, whether it is home-based or governmental. He emphasized the need for both the government and individuals to manage their finances properly for the growth of the country as well as the household.

Giving further insight into the technicalities involved, we have Petra describing financial management as a body of business that is hitherto concerned with the effective and efficient use of borrowed cash, equity capital or any other business fund, and also making the right decision for value addition and profit maximization of an entity. Bradley describes it as the area of business management committed to the judicious use of capital, as well as the careful selection of capital to enable a business organization to move in the direction of achieving its goals. Joseph Massie defines financial management as the operational activities of a business that are responsible for obtaining funds and using them in the most efficient way possible.

Financial management may be divided into Business Finance and Personal Finance, based on the type of finances that are considered. As the names imply, when financial management concerns mainly a business of any form, it is business finance. If it concerns just an individual, it is personal finance. Whatever the type of financial management, its aim or total concept is to manage the funding for day-to-day activities, which can be consumption or investment. Basically, there are two major sources of money available to either a business or an individual. Either you transact with your own money or you make do with someone else's money. Either way, you must make the difficult decision of when and how to deploy money as effectively as possible in such a way that you can successfully maximize profit or benefits and minimize costs, especially if you are using other people's money. There is also the need to consider the possible consequences of your decisions regarding the future and to plan for contingencies. In addition, there is a need for a good financial manager to consider plans for the future, taking into account the consequences, either immediate or future, of such decision making.

Suppose at the end of the month your living expenses are equal to or slightly below your earnings. Then you can use your money as a source of financing. If your income is more than your expenditure, you realize a budget surplus. You can then save this surplus or use it for investment. Either way, you have a potential means for future financial transactions, and at the same time, you are earning more from the money that you saved through investments. However, if at the end, the cumulative result of your expenses surpasses your earnings, there is a budget deficit. In this case, you will need another source of financing (someone else's money). Ideally, most people prefer to avoid financing their expenses with borrowing. Instead, they will seek to create additional income from savings and investments. The techniques for budgeting that will be discussed in this book will help you to achieve this goal.

Over your lifetime, your capability to save will change. This variation depends mainly on the changes in your family structure, your age, your health status and your choice of career. These are the factors that determine whether you experience a budget surplus or suffer a budget deficit in relation to your income and expenditures. The need for external funding (credit or debt) will also change as you save more, control expenses and increase income over time.

Some unexpected developments can suddenly turn an expected budget surplus into a deficit, which forces the individual to end up borrowing. These unexpected events may include the sudden loss of a job, a disease outbreak, war, an economic meltdown and so on. Your ability to understand these sudden changes and know the favorable choices for funding and maintaining cash flows will help you manage your finances through these crises.

Asset procurement is another aspect of financing that we will discuss, as it can be used to create income and limit expenses, especially if it is a long-term asset. These assets can create an increase in value and may even have more value when you are ready to sell them (compared to the initial cost of obtaining them). In most cases, this is the case. However, there are also factors that can help you decide whether to procure a long-term asset or not. These factors include the utility and cost benefit of acquiring such assets. For example, you may find that buying a house is more relevant, effective and useful than renting a confined space when you have a larger family, as it affords you more living space and a healthier life.

Other factors must be examined in financial management planning as well. To start, there is the economic cycle—that is, the rise and fall of market prices due to constant changes in the forces of demand and supply. Others include employment rate and status, financial boom, natural disasters and government policies. In general, these are called macroeconomic factors. The expansion or recession of the

194

economy goes a long way toward affecting your income and expenditures, especially if your earning-power or job is affected. There is also the effect of inflation and deflation (the expected increase or decrease in the value of money or, more subtly, a persistent increase or decrease in market prices) in the value of currency that impacts the interest rates. This means that money that is borrowed or lent has witnessed a change in its value even though the figures have remained the same. As such, the actual value of the original debt might have doubled by the time you repay it.

When these personal and microeconomic factors are incorporated into financial management, making choices becomes a little more complicated. However, if successfully planned, and with these factors taken into consideration, the result gives you a more practical examination of your available alternatives. As such, you can strategize prudently so that you have extra choices open to you in the near future. The difficulty of financial management lies not in its complexity but rather in individual or collective choices. The way you want to live determines the way you finance your lifestyle. In making these decisions, the stakes are high.

Financial management is a project of its own and like every project, it requires planning. The successful implementation of any financial management project centers mainly on the effectiveness of the planning process. In essence, we can say that financial management involves the coordination of financial cash flows in relation to our plans so that we can achieve a desired outcome.

Objectives of financial management

• <u>Wealth Maximization</u>: This is the act of raising the financial value of an organization, individual, group of persons, or entity to its greatest value. This maximization of wealth is the major aim of financial management. Why manage your financial operations and transactions to achieve maximization if not to ensure long-term stability and survival and also prevent bankruptcy? It is more advanced compared to profit maximization because profit maximization means the marginal cost is equal to the marginal revenue, whereas wealth maximization involves a long-term outcome. Wealth maximization ensures that there is the ability to meet both short-term and long-term expectations. Short-term expectations are operational expenses that translate to day-to-day running costs. Long-term expectations are subject to individual personalities and could vary from individual to individual. Meeting short-term goals is necessary in order to achieve long-term goals, but wisdom must also be employed in satisfying those short-term goals. This is because the goal of financial management is to fulfill long-term goals, and someone may be forced to sacrifice some short-term goals as a result.

• Growth: Growth is essential to achieving wealth maximization—which is the primary aim of financial management—and can be accomplished by increasing an individual's current financial capability. For a company, growth is measured by the expansion/diversification rates both internally and externally, which are called internal and external growth, respectively. Internal growth demands that an organization increase its operational facilities such as research, IT, human resources, manufacturing and marketing facilities. Internal growth requires plenty of time in addition to a huge amount of funds. Thus, a lack of time or financial resources can be a major hindrance to an organization's growth.

• Financial Security: To ensure a return on investment or the achievement of one's long-term goal of financial stability and sustainability, financial management maintains the objectives of safety and financial security. To accomplish this, financial risk management and identification of other sources of risk (e.g., accidents, unplanned expenses, natural disasters, health issues and so on) are considered when looking at investments and other day-to-day personal financial activities.

• Profit Maximization: Profit maximization is realized when the marginal cost becomes equal to marginal revenue. It is similar to wealth maximization. This applies to business enterprises or investments made by a person, corporation or nation. Minimization of capital costs helps to raise the profitability of any venture in financial management.

The maximization of one's finances is the main objective of financial management, and growth is essential for increasing one's financial worth. This growth can be achieved through adequate planning, organizing, controlling, monitoring and reviewing of one's day-to-day financial decisions and operations. The outcome of financial management is determined by the quality of the decisions made during financial operations (i.e., planning, savings, investments, expenditures, etc). One incorrect decision could lead to bankruptcy.

Scope of financial management

The following is a brief overview of what financial management entails.

Financial Situation Analysis: This is the part where the organization or individual takes stock of their financial capacity or the state of their present financial situation (i.e., debts, revenue, expenditures, etc). The first stage to overcome a problem is to confess and admit that you have a problem. Then you need to shift from the problem at hand to devising solutions for that problem. The next step is to draw out an estimate of your current financial capability, i.e., debts, revenue, expenses, savings, profits, costs, etc. The estimate must be very thorough and honest because getting the foundation right is necessary for building a strong financial structure.

Creation of Goals: Write down your vision and make it visible such that anyone who reads it knows what is going on. Individuals with precise goals often succeed because they know where they are going and what they are striving for. The first step to making the invisible visible is to quantify it in physical terms and to set goals for yourself that will become your driving force. What do you want to manage if you have no clear view of what your results should look like? How will you know if you have reached your destination? How will you review your successes and failures? The creation of goals is the key to successful financial management. These goals are divided into short term and long term, with the emphasis being on the long-term goals, which are basically financial security and stability. Of course, the short-term goals, or immediate needs, are also imperative to achieving those long-term goals.

Determine a Definite Technique: After having conducted a thorough analysis of the financial position and after goals have been set, decisions must be made concerning the achievement of these goals. Proper planning is done here. Now, one begins to consider control, monitoring and review. Capital structuring is best described as the manner by which organizations finance their total operations and possible growth by using several different sources of financing. The organizations perform deep analysis of equity and debt for both the long and short term. This is done to determine the amount of equity owned in capital and to know the level of external funds to be sourced in financing the company's operations and growth. There are many choices for obtaining these external funds, which may include loans from banks, support from financial firms or funds from shares. (These are deposits from the public which are drawn as bonds.)

For any financial management system that lacks concrete and definite planning, failure is almost guaranteed. There must be a defined and objective plan in place with a large focus on budgeting and assessments. There must also be consideration for sacrifices that will have to be made to create a full understanding of the effect and benefits of opportunity costs. In this process, most organizations plan for their overall operations in such a way that the proper utilization of the available sources of funds is well-executed. This in turn ensures the success of such operations and the growth of the company. In procuring funds, footing the cost of maintenance, paying bills, managing savings and offsetting debts (which are all forms of fund management), some needs may be abandoned or substituted for others. To fully maximize return and utility, a scale of preference is drawn to make the decision to drop one need for the other. However, periodic assessment and gap analysis are done to remain focused on achieving the set organizational goals, either short or long term.

Investment Funds: It is possible to attain a position of success where one reaches a respectable relative realization of one's financial goals and is thereby the proud owner of a small fortune or surplus funds. It is at this point that one begins to exhibit the tendency to be impudent, imprudent and extravagant (the person shows the traits of irrational and fruitless spending). It takes proper discipline and careful consciousness to avoid losing funds at this point. In this case, it is safe to venture into investing such funds. The simplest definition of investment is the allocation of capital (funds) to a business venture to earn profit from the business function and possible appreciation. While it is important to invest because of the possible growth in wealth involved, it is also very important to be careful to avoid losing all of the money that is invested. Bad investments can cause the loss of wealth in the twinkle of an eye, so care is essential in investment. It is a good idea to plan adequately and to be certain about whatever choice you want to make when investing money in the capital and money market.

Strategic financial management

In a world of uncertainties, financial management requires a traditional approach of bounding its subject matters in such a way that one embraces the change process by reassessing the basic assumptions that guide the subject matter of financial management by considering geo-political, economic and social factors. This is what strategic planning showcases—in technical terms, it is the act of specific financial management decision making in relation to the available theories of modern research and further research articles.

What strategic financial management entails is simple. It involves planning specifically and using the already-known principles of financial management systems to pursue and eventually attain set objectives; be it as an individual, group or business, in such a way that the values of all stakeholders involved are maximized. Therefore, in individual financial management, strategic financial management becomes essential; as the already-known principles, methods and techniques of financial management are opened to exploitation by an individual who can choose the one which best suits him or her in terms of managing personal finances. In doing this, the individual must carry out such activities as goal setting, preference management, resources quantification, procedure establishment, and decision making. This means financial decisions will have to be assessed by tracking, monitoring and controlling the variance that occurs in the gap analysis of budgeted and actual performance results. Any problems are identified, and corrective measures are put in place to rectify the anomalies.

In most cases, strategic financial management focuses on long-term success. If there is a craving for short-term gratification, strategic financial management becomes a liability. As a strategy, its key strength lies in discipline and endurance. These are the keys to ensuring the achievement of a long-term goal. In doing this, one must manage his or her assets and liabilities, earnings and expenses, savings and investments, and any other financial transaction that needs to be evaluated. Whether it is a short or long-term goal, the essence is to realize such goals with effective maximization of profit. Sacrifices are made, especially in adjusting short-term goals to achieve a more profitable long-term objective. Also, a person must restructure some, if not most, of his or her financial transactions. Such structured spending might come in the form of reducing unnecessary and addictive spending that is transacted mostly in the short term.

Financial management decisions for a firm

Capital budgeting is the process by which financiers plan and manage the long-term investment of organizations to determine whether such investments are feasible. Such investments could lead to the development of a new product, purchase of new machinery, establishment of a new factory or the carrying out of specific research. In summary, it is the process of managing key capital investment and expenses. The estimate of the financial (capital) requirement of a firm is one of the major roles of the finance manager. To make this estimate, he or she must factor in the project's expected costs, expected profits, both current and future policies that may affect the project, and any other future projects that may also affect it. If the estimate is made in a structured manner, the earning capacity of such an organization can increase greatly.

The functions of capital budgeting involve decisions about:

- Whether to abandon or continue existing projects.
- The commencement of a new project.
- The certainty of replacing existing assets with new ones.
- The financing of research and development.

Decision making in capital budgeting is strictly for the long term. A firm must decide whether to commit its funds to the acquisition of long-term assets or the financing of a process with expectations of a possible future benefit in the maximization of wealth over a given period. The firm must make these decisions to affect its value by way of influencing the growth and risk of such value.

To fully understand the concept of capital budgeting, one must combine a series of topics that cover disciplines such as mathematics, economics, financial accounting and management engineering, control techniques and marketing. This helps to effectively manage the capital budgeting process. A standard capital budgeting program entails proper planning, policy making and programming. In broader categorization, a capital budgeting program incorporates project generation, evaluations, selection and execution. However, more processes may be included to boost its effectiveness and success.

Techniques for evaluation in capital budgeting

Evaluation is an important process to carry out after creating and specifying a project so that the project manager can determine the actual performance of the project against the budgeted parameters. Here, a comparison is made between actual figures and the figures recorded in the budget for the project to ensure that its scope is maintained at positive costs. It is also essential to carry out an evaluation to assess whether the project is returning the expected earnings or the expected net cash inflow that was planned according to the budget. If these are not ascertained or are found to be negative, the decision to effect proper corrections or even discontinue the project can be made to ensure that capital is not eventually lost.

A method of conducting evaluations

Evaluation techniques must meet the objective of determining the success of a capital investment project by comparing the elements of the planned budget against the elements of the project's actual performance. There are several ways of doing this, and they are discussed under two major headings. However, the size of the firm's projects can sometimes determine the method adopted.

1. Discounted Cash Flow Techniques

2. Non-Discounted Cash Flow Techniques

Discounted cash flow techniques consider the time value in estimating calculations. With this technique, there are two methods of evaluating a project performance. The first is the Net Present Value (NPV) evaluation method, which is calculated by taking the difference between net present capital expenses and net present capital earnings. The second method is the Internal Rate of Return Method (IRR), which is preferred by most organizations and financiers because of their familiarity with the rate of return instead of the actual monetary value.

The non-discounted cash flow technique approaches that can be taken are the Accounting Rate of Return approach and the Payback Period Method. These techniques are explained below.

1. Payback Period Method:
   This approach does not consider the value of money over time. It stems from the belief that when money is spent on a capital investment, it would surely yield its equivalent value over a certain period of years. The number of years it would take to get back the original investment is estimated. The point at which the total money earned or generated is equal to that spent on the project is the payback period. This assumes that the project generates money over its life span or period of existence. Therefore, when considering projects on which to embark, it is wiser to choose the one which generates its estimated total cost in the shortest possible time.

   Advantages of the Payback Method
   - It ensures that project investments are recovered quickly.
   - The concept is quite easy to grasp.
   - It is especially required when investing or taking on projects in which the total estimated cost is unpredictable
   - It can be easily communicated to the other members of the team.
   - It does not require complex calculation.

   Disadvantages of the Payback Method

- It does not take real-life occurrences into consideration. The method assumes we operate in an ideal world, taking only the assets into consideration.
- It considers only the total earnings of that project without considering capital wastage and the project's economic life.
- This method is inflexible and quite delicate. A change, albeit small, in any factor might considerably affect the payback period.
- It assumes that liquidity is the aim of all capital expenses and decisions.
- It does not consider the time value of money, focusing only on when the returns equal the costs.
- It disregards any other income generated after the set payback period, which can be confusing when budget decisions are being made.

2. Accounting Rate of Return Method (ARR):
   This is a mathematical ratio that compares the annual accounting profit to the total cost of investment. This approach is commonly used with the payback method described above, to analyze how profitable an investment would eventually be. It is known by other names, like Return on Investment, the Financial Statement Method or the Unadjusted Rate of Return Method.

   This approach uses the operating earnings of the business from the Profit and Loss account. This allows us to understand what the annual cash flow is like. When we have calculated the annual profit, (i.e., profits minus taxes) we then divide it by the estimated total cost of the investment. The projects are then arranged in descending order starting with projects with the highest yields. Eventually, those with the lowest estimated yields are removed.

Conclusion

Congratulations on completing this book!

I hope this book was able to help you learn more about minimalism and financial management.

The next step is to share with others what you have learned.

Finally, if you enjoyed this book, I'd like to ask you for a favor. Would you be kind enough to leave a positive review for this book on Amazon? It would be greatly appreciated!

Thank you and good luck!

Made in the USA
Columbia, SC
06 June 2018